Meeting the Mandate:
Renewing the College and Departmental Curriculum

by William Toombs and William Tierney

ASHE-ERIC Higher Education Report No. 6, 1991

Prepared by

Clearinghouse on Higher Education
The George Washington University

In cooperation with

Association for the Study
of Higher Education

Published by

School of Education and Human Development
The George Washington University

Jonathan D. Fife, Series Editor

Cite as
Toombs, William, and William Tierney. 1991. *Meeting the Mandate: Renewing the College and Departmental Curriculum.* ASHE-ERIC Higher Education Report No. 6. Washington, D.C.: The George Washington University, School of Education and Human Development.

Library of Congress Catalog Card Number 92-80932
ISSN 0884-0040
ISBN 1-878380-11-7

Managing Editor: Bryan Hollister
Manuscript Editor: Barbara Fishel, Editech
Cover design by Michael David Brown, Rockville, Maryland

The ERIC Clearinghouse on Higher Education invites individuals to submit proposals for writing monographs for the *ASHE-ERIC Higher Education Report* series. Proposals must include:
1. A detailed manuscript proposal of not more than five pages.
2. A chapter-by-chapter outline.
3. A 75-word summary to be used by several review committees for the initial screening and rating of each proposal.
4. A vita and a writing sample.

ERIC Clearinghouse on Higher Education
School of Education and Human Development
The George Washington University
One Dupont Circle, Suite 630
Washington, DC 20036-1183

This publication was prepared partially with funding from the Office of Educational Research and Improvement, U.S. Department of Education, under contract no. ED RI-88-062014. The opinions expressed in this report do not necessarily reflect the positions or policies of OERI or the Department.

EXECUTIVE SUMMARY

In the grain and chaff of criticism and analysis that have fallen on colleges and universities in the past decade are several new and compelling issues. To accommodate diverse races and ethnic traditions and both genders, to incorporate global perspectives on the environment and exchange among nations, and to deal more effectively with the human dimensions of the educational equation are distinctive challenges. Bound into the fabric of the larger society by their importance and complexity, they take on the qualities of mandates. For education, these contemporary demands differ in essential ways from the press of new knowledge or the expansion of the business and professional sectors, drivers of the 1970s and 1980s. They transcend the disciplines without diminishing their value and introduce considerations that have not been faced before in their full complexity.

Even though other sectors of society share the mandates—political policy makers, leaders in the justice system, and managers in corporate practice, for example—it is in the undergraduate curriculum that many of the issues come together for academics. It is important to recognize that the collegiate experience has its own dimensions and its own functions. In the fullest sense, the curriculum is intended to serve all students by means of an experience that has enough unity to sustain a common discourse among the best trained and educated. If students are to be in tune with a world few of their mentors have known, the course of study will have to be changed in fundamental ways still to be determined, discovered, or made.

At least five conditions for changing the curriculum can be identified, as much in terms of direction as specifics. First, a firmer grasp is needed on what the curriculum is as an idea, what language can describe it, and at what levels it operates. The concept of design and a pragmatic terminology give an operational definition. Second, the flood of criticism, dissection, recommendation, and interpretation visited on the collegiate curriculum merits a careful review. Third, the need is continuous for modest self-analysis dealing with what the academic profession is and what its condition of practice should be. Fourth, because we know so little about what the solutions might be, a longer perspective is needed. The mode of change will be comprehensive, calling for a thorough exploration of the issues as well as attention to bases of action.

Finally, the management of transforming change in the curriculum brings to the fore a pronounced need for wider understanding of the organization and its content. Together these factors point toward a two-stage process for opening curricular change to the mandates. The preparatory stage emphasizes legitimation of substance and method, exploration to generate understanding, and negotiation. Then the central task becomes one of moving to action in ways that recognize the shape of change and the forces of culture within which it moves.

ADVISORY BOARD

CONSULTING EDITORS

Paula Y. Bagasao
University of California System

Rose R. Bell
New School for Social Research

Louis W. Bender
Florida State University

David G. Brown
University of North Carolina–Asheville

Clifton F. Conrad
University of Wisconsin–Madison

James Cooper
FIPSE College Teaching Project

Richard A. Couto
Tennessee State University

Donald F. Dansereau
Texas Christian University

Peter Frederick
Wabash College

Mildred Garcia
Montclair State College

Virginia N. Gordon
Ohio State University

Wesley R. Habley
American College Testing

Michael L. Hanes
West Chester University

Dianne Horgan
Memphis State University

John L. Howarth
Private Consultant

Susan Jeffords
University of Washington

Greg Johnson
Harvard College

Margaret C. King
Schenectady County Community College

Joseph Lowman
University of North Carolina

Jean MacGregor
Evergreen State College

Christine Maitland
National Education Association

Richard Morrill
Centre College

Laura I. Rendón
North Carolina State University

R. Eugene Rice
Antioch University

Richard Robbins
State University of New York–Plattsburg

Carol F. Stoel
American Association for Higher Education

Susan Stroud
Brown University

Stuart Suss
City University of New York–Kingsborough

Marilla D. Svinicki
University of Texas–Austin

Elizabeth Watson
California State University–Humboldt

Janice Weinman
The College Board

William R. Whipple
University of Maine

Roger B. Winston
University of Georgia

REVIEW PANEL

Charles Adams
University of Massachusetts–Amherst

Louis Albert
American Association for Higher Education

Richard Alfred
University of Michigan

Philip G. Altbach
State University of New York–Buffalo

Marilyn J. Amey
University of Kansas

Louis C. Attinasi, Jr.
University of Houston

Robert J. Barak
Iowa State Board of Regents

Alan Bayer
Virginia Polytechnic Institute and State University

John P. Bean
Indiana University

Louis W. Bender
Florida State University

John M. Braxton
Syracuse University

Peter McE. Buchanan
Council for Advancement and
    Support of Education

John A. Centra
Syracuse University

Arthur W. Chickering
George Mason University

Shirley M. Clark
Oregon State System of Higher Education

Darrel A. Clowes
Virginia Polytechnic Institute and State University

John W. Creswell
University of Nebraska–Lincoln

CONTENTS

FOREWORD

The call to review and redirect the college curriculum originates from the sense that the curriculum is no longer achieving its intended purpose. Central to curriculum review is development of a clear understanding of the curriculum's vision and mission. It is not sufficient to make observations about the increased diversity of students or recount the technological and scientific changes sweeping through a particular discipline without showing how such factors affect the process *and* intended outcomes of a college education.

The college curriculum is more than just a collection of courses that a student puts together like so many graduation stamps until enough are collected to qualify for a diploma. It should be a conceptual framework that includes consideration of at least the following questions:

- *What are students' educational expectations?* While students likely do not know specifically what courses or body of knowledge appropriately makes up their program of study, they do have expectations for specific outcomes—and those outcomes should be respected and considered during design of the curriculum. Ignoring these expectations or withholding the truth from students (such as the types of jobs and starting salaries available for program graduates) is tantamount to academic fraud.
- *What is the sum body of knowledge making up a particular discipline, profession, or area of study?* Unless a curricular area periodically assesses the total knowledge base, the program will inevitably contain only those courses within the expertise of the current faculty. While this approach can sometimes be more than adequate, the knowledge offered through a curriculum should not be left to chance. If the knowledge base of a curricular area is periodically reviewed, the faculty can make conscious, informed decisions about what is being made available to students and not allow the quality of the curriculum to be determined by uncontrolled changing of faculty interests, personalities, or availability.
- *What are society's expectations for outcomes?* All colleges receive some public support. Most institutions, through student aid, categorical grants, or direct support, receive a great deal of public assistance. Why? Because colleges add value to society. Unfortunately, this value often cannot be measured. But the expectations employers have

for college graduates *are* measurable—and they are being poorly met. Society's support of higher education is largely determined by how satisfied employers and voters are with the quality of graduates. And the willingness of state and local governments to withhold funds is an indication of dissatisfaction!

As long as these three precepts are continually included as part of its vision and mission, the college and departmental curricula can be renewed successfully and effectively.

William Toombs, professor emeritus, and William Tierney, associate professor and senior research associate, both of the Center for the Study of Higher Education at The Pennsylvania State University, present the background, theory, and process of curricular change in this monograph. They discuss current academic and professional curricular practices, the curricular debate, reconceptualization, analysis of the curriculum, and the planning and implementation of organizational and curricular change, stressing the concept of "transformation," both of the curriculum and in the thinking that designs it.

What cannot be overlooked is that renewing college and departmental curricula is not a process but a result. The process leading to renewal takes place with incremental steps, each guided by a long-range vision. That vision must transcend the day-to-day restrictions of individual faculty members and become the wisdom of the collective whole—faculty, students, and society in general. This report is a step toward development of such a vision.

Jonathan D. Fife
Series Editor, Professor, and Director, ERIC Clearinghouse
    on Higher Education
The George Washington University

ACKNOWLEDGMENTS

This publication was prepared partially with funding from the Lilly Endowment and from the U.S. Department of Education's Office of Educational Research and Improvement Grant No. R117G10037. Indirectly, projects supported by the Exxon Education Foundation and the Challenge Grant program of New Jersey contributed to the analysis.

INTRODUCTION

A Place in History

Apocalypse or Golden Age. The choice is ours. As we approach the beginning of the third millennium, the way we address that question will define what it means to be human (Naisbitt and Aburdene 1990, p. xxiv).

Times were to grow worse over the next fifty-odd years until at some imperceptible moment, by some mysterious chemistry, energies were refreshed, ideas broke out of the mold . . . into new realms and humanity found itself redirected (Tuchman 1978, p. 581).

> **Wise choices are, in fact, the central challenge for the curriculum.**

These quotations, the first on the eve of the 21st century, the other recounting the threshold of the 15th, hold two messages. First, they tell us of an abiding challenge to higher learning: forever a search for the mysterious chemistry that refreshes energies and for clues that mark the imperceptible moment, thus to aid in that risky choice. The second, more immediate in its implications, is that the way we address that question is a product of our own devising. The product varies from age to age—these days from decade to decade—but more than ever before choices become realities. Wise choices are, in fact, the central challenge for the curriculum.

Even without the detailed documentation provided (see, e.g., Apple 1983; Brentlinger 1986; Kidder 1987; Naisbitt and Aburdene 1990; Williams 1986), we can see that the objective of the search for the next generation is the creation of a pluralistic society rich in human values and set in a global community, a world of individualism *and* diversity. To do so calls for new levels of understanding and acceptance (Ornstein and Ehrlich 1989). Education is good at activating understanding but limited in its capacity to build acceptance.

Unfinished Business

Unfinished business of the present and recent past in science, management, and technology still challenges the academic world, but the essence of the search now is for a better comprehension of the human terms in the equation—seeking to enhance one's understanding of humanity and society, according to Kenyon College's catalog. In the framework of the curriculum, the search takes three forms: modification, integration, and transformation.

Each form of change is considered in the following sections, but most of this monograph is directed toward transformation and the importance of the curriculum in the search. Before discussing the most intriguing idea, transformation, however, one should take note of three puzzling themes that persist in the writing and reporting on the curriculum.

First, the whole idea of a curriculum, the concept itself, is so loosely defined as to be unbound. Subsequent pages analyze this problem and develop the notion of curriculum as a problem in design. The terms used to describe the curriculum and its components are limited and unsystematic, a serious handicap to professional practice that calls for remedies. One approach to both the concept and the terminology is presented in the section titled "Definitions and Reference Points."

Second, pressures on the collegiate curriculum are so numerous and varied that the critics, choices, and mandates merit review ("Meeting Mandates" and "Forces of Change"). "The Nature of Professional Practice" considers the faculty perspective on the curriculum.

Third, the process of framing and managing curricular change within an established organization is not well understood, but "The Process of Analysis" explores ways to implement such change. Finally, organizational change is addressed in "Managing Change in the Curriculum."

A Primary Audience

A primary audience is the teaching faculty as well as department heads, deans, provosts, and vice presidents, that is, all who take seriously their shared responsibility for the events that make up an undergraduate program of learning—a curriculum—not just classes. More specifically, the intended audiences are faculty members joined in collaborative groups to look into a whole program—conditions found in committees, task forces, teams, or study groups.

Other audiences for whom the ideas could be useful are those attending to the overall patterns of teaching and learning, whether at the level of a degree program, an institution, a system, or a collection of similar programs. Thus, regional and professional accreditation teams will find something of value. Board members, advisory committees, and staff members—anyone who is open to a broader understanding and new perspectives on accountability for learning—will find this approach useful.

The line of argument is straightforward and constructed around two main ideas:

1. *The curriculum is a sophisticated artifact* that offers the best vehicle for addressing the challenges of diversity, the substance of criticism, the evolving structure of knowledge, the dynamics of students' choices, and rising costs.
2. *Conditions today call for change of a special kind* beyond our more familiar notions of modification and reform.

The idea of "transformation" has been selected to signify the new scope of change. The process of change has two phases, one setting up the framework for transformation, the other addressing directly the process of organizational change. Before undertaking a transformation, however, the curriculum must be better defined, more accurately described, and elevated as a key concern of professional practice. The substance of criticism and experimentation in the last decade merits examination.

Finally, this monograph sets forth distinct priorities and definite points of view that are intended to bring order to the discourse, not to foreclose other views and opinions or lay claim to a completely integrated system of thought and action, a single inviolable instrument. It is one contribution among many toward solving the enigma of the curriculum. Curricular issues are hard issues—hard to define, hard to analyze, and hard to negotiate—but they are still the heart of the enterprise. Readers are urged to take what fits, modify freely, discuss even more freely, dissent at will, and find their own application.

MEETING MANDATES

Challenges and the Curriculum
Generating new organizations
Challenges to and changes in the curriculum are continuous. Variations in the challenges and changes come largely in how the academy responds. Over the past several decades, the way we address the questions of expansion and differentiation in the U.S. postsecondary system has been to invent new institutional forms. The community college movement, the transformation of teachers colleges into comprehensive universities, and the rapid rise of proprietary schools carried forward the democratization of opportunity. U.S. graduate schools and the refinement of professional schools within universities provided organizational devices for the production of highly trained people, the growth of research, and the introduction of new relationships with industry and government. Experiments with organizational approaches continue: Nova University and its counterparts, adult and continuing education programs, distance learning, and joint enterprises among universities all stand as examples. So far, we have met the press of specialized knowledge and techniques, massive increases in enrollments, and the differentiation of social functions mainly by creating new departments, schools, divisions, or institutions and by encouraging them to make new curricula. Traditionally, the United States has preferred to invent new organizations, not to reform programs (Toombs and Escala 1986).

But it is doubtful that merely adding new kinds of institutions can accommodate the prospective complexity.

Students' choices
One change that has the qualities of a curricular mandate is the awesome shift in students' elections of major field. It is surprising that the consequences for academic communities have been discussed so little, but that fact could be attributable to the myopia of the disciplines. What does it mean when the accounting department becomes larger than the English department in seven years? When the computer science department doubles every three years but history decreases by a third? The shift in students' preferences was anticipated more than three decades ago: "The sheer fact of tremendous increase in enrollments has unsettled the traditional tacit treaties among the disciplines" (Riesman 1956, p. 79). The forces at work here are products of a larger, continuous phenomenon, a rapidly moving economy, and a new social contract.

In a knowledge-based, information-rich society, the ways in which ideas are translated into use stimulate both students' choices and changes in the disciplinary structure. The prospect in view is a dynamic curriculum that is flexible in size and content and reaches beyond an architectonic view of knowledge. The alternative of a hyperspecialized organizational structure now carries weaker logic for the needs of students than it did two decades ago.

Cost creep

A different kind of influence on organizational options comes from the rising costs of learning and its supporting dimensions. Computer technology, library services, audiovisual materials, office services, and publication are entwined with the curriculum, differing across programs. By custom, departments and deans' offices are the management loci for budgeting. But the classroom, laboratory, and library are commanding more and more supplies, equipment, services, and facilities. The cost of keeping and transmitting knowledge increases just as the more visible costs of generating knowledge through research rise. In short, the curriculum itself is a major cost center.

Evidence suggests that about one in eight institutions is not keeping up with and in fact decreased educational and general expenditures (El-Khawas 1987). The strictures appear to have increased, but they are less often discussed, a condition that promises an "educational austerity" for new ideas (Wharton 1979). Creating new units is now a costly solution to mandates for change.

The principal mandate for higher education

A principal mandate for higher education is to navigate the cultural crosscurrents surging in the country's value structure. Banners of the 1960s and 1970s have multiplied into dozens of pennants, each marching with its own rationale. Installing each in a separate organization can only foment separatism and contention that deny a democratic consensus.

But in any case, many of those diverse interests belong together. To become truly pluralistic and not simply a balkanized society, we must find means to incorporate diversity around a common human ground within our institutions. Recent events in Yugoslavia remind us vividly and tragically what the metaphor "balkanized" signifies. Colleges and universities are high on the list. Looking toward curriculum at the turn of the century, one author identified the sources of difficulty as increasing conflict from a polarization of interests, tensions as business and industry make direct demands on the curriculum, externally controlled, mission-specific funding, and a view of curriculum development as a social act (Apple 1983).

If organizational proliferation is limited by cost and the very complexity of issues, then changing the curriculum in colleges and universities is an obvious medium for addressing concerns. Because the college curriculum has the qualities of a zero-sum game, any transformation of the curriculum is likely to be accompanied by reverberating adjustments to traditional forms of organization.

Three Forms of Curricular Change
Challenges to the curriculum have never been in short supply. Often they run in opposite directions and carry threats of ideological collision. It is up to faculties to find—more commonly to *make*—a balanced curriculum out of these challenges. Two modes are familiar—modification and integration; one is new—curricular transformation.

One is to modify the conditions of learning, re-forming the curriculum and accounting for new knowledge. Disciplines and professional fields are continuously called on to adapt courses and programs to fit emerging theory, technique, practice, and epistemology. Studies of curricular history show that one way to deal with the differentiation of knowledge has been "compartmentalization" (Hopmann 1991, p. 4). This approach can be traced to the late decades of the last century, paralleling the entrance into the curriculum of the natural sciences with an emphasis on positivism, reductionism, and specialization (Clark 1983). In modifying the conditions of learning, the issues of importance are setting boundaries and defining interrelationships among the disciplines, what the students of curricular history at the University of Kiel refer to as "segmentation" (Hopmann 1991, p. 9). In the process of modification, goals can be defined and the parties of interest known, usually a few departments, so the process of change can follow familiar processes of planned change.

Familiar though this response to new knowledge might be, a growing view holds that a postmodern era could be upon us and that other modes are needed. Ideas such as "open systems," complexity theory, and theories of change by saltation require curricular responses we are not yet prepared to offer (Doll 1989, p. 251). Modification is, nevertheless, the kind of curricular change we know most about.

A second kind of curricular change, a reaction to reductionist philosophies and specialization, is integration. The search for unity in knowledge, a proper scope to studies, and linkage within the curriculum has a long history. The tradition is marked by rich discourse and imaginative approaches to pedagogy and the design of curricula. The goal of attaining a sense of unity, of synthesis, from the fragmented structure of disciplinary specialties comes from two roots.

Older integrators emphasized the unity of "truth" and intellectual commitment whatever the field of study. "The university has locked itself into methodologies that preclude serious consideration of certain regions of reality. The central curricular issue of our age is whether the university is grounded in an epistemology that allows for open rather than constricted vision" (Huston Smith, cited in Clark and Wawrytko 1990, p. 123). A second argument for integration is found in the challenge to bridge the gap between the pattern of learning and the nature of the active world. "The curriculum bears little connection to contemporary reality, and even when it does, it is in such a fragmented form that little useful understanding is possible" (p. 2). The goal of an integrated curriculum has been discussed at conferences and received major emphasis in the studies of the Carnegie Foundation over the past decade (Boyer 1987). Efforts to include the substance of liberal learning into professional preparation offer another example of integrative change; an ambitious undertaking at Syracuse University reflects a wide range of analysis (Marsh 1988).

Proposals for integrated learning usually encompass only a segment of the total curriculum, one constellation of courses or one certification program. The media for integration are fairly well accepted and run along the lines of interdisciplinary offerings or comprehensive pedagogies, such as senior seminars or broad-gauged projects. If goals are known, then interested parties can be designated, the vehicles for change identified, and the regular planning processes followed.

Curricular transformation is the third kind of mandated change. Like the other two, it offers a modality by which the issues can be described, examined, negotiated, and accommodated. But transformation is very different from the other two processes. The issues are new and to a degree undefined, leaving open the subject of goals or even outcomes. The scope of concern is wider, the stake holders more numerous, and the appropriate media for action not yet known. Even though the mandate might be clear, the process of curricular change and the breadth and depth of the challenges in such a setting are different and somewhat unfamiliar, leading to the concentration in much of this analysis on transforming influences in the curriculum.

The choice of "transform" over the more popular "reform" is a considered decision. Reform denotes a return to a natural or normal state. It connotes a condition in which the direction of change and the final state are known. Transform, however, connotes a metamorphosis (see, in addition to much of the feminist literature, Conrad and Haworth 1991; Conrad and Pratt 1983). What the authors have tried to do here is to fix the concept in terms of action. In the words of one experienced participant, "A transformation in thinking" should precede curricular reorganization (Andersen 1988, p. 48).

A second argument for integration is found in the challenge to bridge the gap between the pattern of learning and the nature of the active world.

Those issues that press toward curricular transformation share several attributes. Each set poses questions that cannot be fully answered by disciplines and professional areas as they are now conducted. Each presents penetrating questions of values that carry strong political overtones. Each offers little help in pointing toward an acceptable pedagogy or, for that matter, a research agenda or charter for public service. Now at the forefront are questions of gender equity, ethnicity, internationalism or multiculturalism, ethics and social responsibility, and environmentalism.

In short, what is to be done on these topics, by whom, and how are all open to exploration. Each holds the prospect of a transforming change in the curriculum, not simply modification or integration. Matters of such scope are best addressed by a full examination of how academics conceive their role and how the curriculum itself is defined, analyzed, and changed. But before taking up these details, a few basic assumptions are in order.

An Educational Premise
An educational premise underlying this monograph is the view that a curriculum is an act of collective response by a collegiate faculty. It is an expression of intellectual account-

ability as a faculty responds to external factors—society's expectations and changes in knowledge—and to internal factors, such as students' needs. That response might be imaginative or creative, merely pedestrian, or even servile. At its best, it is the product of an independent reading by an academic community of what is needed at a particular time and an educational expression of that need. In more sophisticated terms:

> *The University must now take on that overall cybernetic function of analyzing in its own way the needs of society and feeding back that information in the form of education programs* (CERI/OECD 1972).

History and tradition offer only limited help with that cybernetic function. Each curriculum has a history, but the force of history operates as an external stimulus, not an internal dynamic for the curriculum itself.

> *It is tempting to describe changes in a curriculum as historically sequential but that would be misleading. . . . The history of education is as much a story of culture and institutions as of ideas* (Rothblatt 1988, p. 12).

This idea is presented well in the introduction to a series of historical studies:

> *Every institution partly reflects the social, economic, and political system, but partly also it lives a life of its own, independent of the interests and beliefs of the community. . . . What is abundantly clear is that the response of the university to external change has been neither simple nor immediate. . . . Nor does the history of the university lend any support to theories about its simple function to inculcate established values and transmit established cultural norms. . . . The university has not been a Parsonian functionalist institution responding slavishly to social needs. Nor has it been a Marxist superstructure, automatically providing the ideological props for the group that currently controls the means of production* (Stone 1974, p. v).

And this approach has practical consequences:

After a number of years of work in curriculum revision involving women's studies, I found that my colleagues and I were frequently making judgments without having made the grounds of our judgments explicit (McIntosh 1983).

What is studied, how, and why must be constructed and reconstructed from the interplay of the academy and the world outside. History and philosophy provide only breadth and insight, not direct guidance. The fundamental accountability of academics is for the way they translate the forces at work in that larger world into the substance of the collegiate curriculum—in short, where they stand (Eberle 1974).

DEFINITIONS AND REFERENCE POINTS

Setting Boundaries

If the curriculum is to be the instrument of change, its meanings and operational terms must be clearer than they are currently. For all its frivolous Latin roots, the larger meanings of "curriculum" do not spring from the literal meaning, a race-course, but from the practical, chilly, Calvinist climate of Scotland. Medieval universities and colleges derived their power not from teaching, research, or a coherent program of studies but from the right to certify and examine. Historical accounts show us that studies on the continent and in England were little more than loose congeries of subjects grouped around faculty members. Canon law, theology, and civil law predominated. The period of study was of indeterminate length, with the professor and examiners the arbiters.

> How long a student remained part of the corporation of "professeurs" depended on a number of factors. . . . The duration depended primarily on a student's choice of professor or university, for . . . the period of residence demanded of graduands could vary significantly from faculty to faculty and from institution to institution (Brockliss 1987, p. 55).

In Spain, students often attended university only a year or two, until they landed a preferment in the hierarchy of civil or church administration (Kagan 1975, p. 355). The fortunes, enrollments, and subjects in French and German universities were "continually threatened by the brooding, 'protective' presence of spiritual and temporal powers" (Brockliss 1987, p. 444). Only the Scottish universities adopted the modern usage for "curriculum." The earliest recorded reference, at the University of Glasgow in 1643, identifies a "curriculum quinque annorum." The term kept its meaning, and the Glasgow calendar of 1829 refers to "the curriculum of students who mean to take degrees in Surgery to be three years" (Oxford University 1971).

Scottish usage did not spread widely or rapidly. In the normal course of events, once a useful concept is introduced, the term is elaborated, invested with specific meanings, and articulated as part of the technical terminology. For whatever reason, those events never quite happened with the idea of a curriculum. It is not accidental that the two settings where the notion of a curriculum did persist were Scotland and the

United States. Scottish learneds and divines populated the colonial universities in America. They brought with them the influences of the Scottish Enlightenment, stern in its theology and orderly in its views of education.

> *The colonial colleges, founded like the lower schools to preserve tradition and transmit culture, had become mildly innovative in spite of themselves. . . . Colonial colleges consequently often looked for precedent and advice to the more lively Scottish universities and the far more innovative Dissenting academies of England* (May 1976, p. 33).

With "moral philosophy" at the peak of the curriculum, these influences continued well into the 19th century.

> *It is not hard to understand the conquest of academic America in the early 19th century by the philosophy of Common Sense. It was enlightened, moderate, practical, and easy to teach. It could be used to sustain or validate any set of ideas, but was in fact associated with the Moderate Enlightenment and Moderate Calvinism. It was never anti-scientific nor obscurantist, never cynical, and it opened no doors to intellectual or moral chaos* (May 1976, p. 346).

In the United States, the development of a *structure* for the curriculum, the "macrodimension" of the teaching-learning experience, proceeded rapidly. The expansion and differentiation of the natural sciences, the "elective principle [that] led to the gradual elimination of the old curriculum and to the success of the new scholarly disciplines and professional studies" (Ben-David 1972, p. 58), and the more sophisticated organization of American universities all contributed to the evolution of an orderly, phased schedule of studies (Ben-David 1977, p. 77). Structural features of the curriculum were standardized: the adoption of "Carnegie credits" in high schools that carried over into colleges, and agreement on course nomenclature, degrees, and academic dress. "Much of the writing on the curriculum . . . in the U.S. was . . . administrative and managerial in emphasis," however (Squires 1990, p. 1; see also Reid 1986, p. 159).

In contrast to the growth of curricular structure, the passage of the idea—the concept of what the realm of the curriculum might be—became highly diffused, and two consequences of this vague historical track are with us still. First, the curriculum as a concept, as a discrete idea, is almost without boundaries. It can mean anything from the "bundle" of programs an institution offers to the individual experience of a particular student. Second, systematic description, that is, an orderly, technical terminology that will enhance insights on practice and is a means of linking ideas to application, has not developed. "What we appear to lack . . . is a general vocabulary or framework for understanding the nature of knowledge and skills across university disciplines" (Donald 1986, p. 267). Often faculty at work on the curriculum are forced to invent their own labels to describe what they do.

The idea of a curriculum has been differentiated across a wide range of meanings. One basic view is that curriculum is "what is taught" (Squires 1990). A narrow view holds that curriculum is "the body of courses that present knowledge, principles, values, and skills that are the intended consequences of formal education" (Levine 1981). And the broad view holds that "the curriculum . . . will have to be conceived as the name for the total active life of each person in college" (Taylor 1950, p. 220). Even the set of choices from which the curriculum can be defined is broad.

Some see a split in the definition.

It is important at the outset to distinguish clearly between two meanings of the term "curriculum." The word [can] connote either formal structural arrangements or the substance of what is being taught. (To be sure, the relations between form and substance, here as always, are complex.) (Veysey 1973, p. 73).

Others find evidence of six uses:

1. A college's—or program's—mission, purpose, or collective expression of what is important for students to learn;
2. A set of experiences that some authorities believe all students should have;
3. The set of courses offered to students;
4. The set of courses students actually elect from those available;
5. The content of a specific discipline; and
6. The time and credit frame in which the college provides education (Stark and Lowther 1986, p. 45).

The distinction between structure and concept is important in light of the preemptive administrative interest and faculty neglect of the idea. Most faculty would side with the notion that "the structural aspects of the curriculum have much less to do with the quality of an education than is often believed. Quality instead is more importantly linked to matters of substance" (Veysey 1973, p. 22). Or they would subscribe to the view that "all arguments of detail about the curriculum are absolutely pointless. . . . Arguments of principle, centering on what to do instead of lining up courses end to end until graduation, might be helpful" (Caws 1974, p. 24).

A result of this diffusion is recorded in faculty interviews showing how difficult it is for faculty members to get much beyond their own courses in thinking about the curriculum (Stark et al. 1988, p. 85). Most analysts find it chaotic as well. This disorder is a product of many factors:

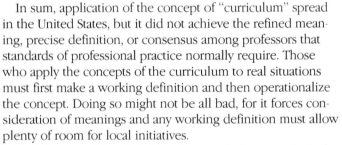

> *The curricular disarray constitutes a major artifact that permits several inferences. It testifies to the loss of confidence among faculty. It testifies to the enlargement of popular functions. . . . And it provides archeological evidence of the vast transformation of the amount and shape of knowledge—what there is to teach—over the past century* (Bowen 1977, p. 413).

In sum, application of the concept of "curriculum" spread in the United States, but it did not achieve the refined meaning, precise definition, or consensus among professors that standards of professional practice normally require. Those who apply the concepts of the curriculum to real situations must first make a working definition and then operationalize the concept. Doing so might not be all bad, for it forces consideration of meanings and any working definition must allow plenty of room for local initiatives.

Building a working definition fortunately has recent scholarly compilations of definitions to draw on (see Conrad 1978, 1985b for a comparative analysis; Dressel 1971 for a classic work on reconciling tensions; Eisner and Vallance 1974 for a discussion of five of the essential conflicts that surface in curricular work; Mayhew and Ford 1971 for the compilation of a range of views around the theme that "the curriculum is a struggle to accommodate many competing issues" [p. 5]; and Stark and Lowther 1986 for a full review of definitions and the literature that supports them, including a review of the use in kindergarten through grade 12 and an articulated schema of the major topics that bear on the curriculum). It is interesting, perhaps a sign of progress, to find that many of the earlier working definitions of, say, 20 years ago tried to incorporate as many dimensions of study as possible into the definition of curriculum, while later definitions have tended to focus on coherence across a more limited scope.

A working definition can be constructed around several common concepts. First, the curriculum as a *plan for learning* is well developed (see Stark et al. 1988), based on a comprehensive analysis of the literature on the subject. Further field research among faculty led back to the "course" and course planning as the fundamental component of such a plan, not the curriculum. Second, the curriculum can be seen as an *instructional system,* another well-developed approach (see Diamond 1989 for both theoretical and practical aspects of sustaining a highly systematic program of action). Third, the concept of system has been extended to consider the curriculum as a *major subsystem of the university,* thus opening analysis of the inputs and outcomes (Conrad 1978). This approach can be characterized as "systemic curricular planning." Fourth, the idea of the curriculum as a *medium of student development* has been explored and developed in some of the most compelling literature of higher education (see Chickering 1981; Chickering et al. 1977; Cross and McCartan 1984; Gamson et al. 1984; and Sanford 1962, among others). Fifth, strong traditional orientations to the curriculum as an *analog to the structure of knowledge* persist in "essentialist" approaches and in contemporary reinterpretations (Bell 1966; Hirst 1974; Phenix 1964).

Useful but more instrumental or prescriptive aids to defining curriculum also are widely found in the literature. Perhaps the simplest framework for looking at the curriculum is provided by four penetrating questions about purpose, content, organization, and evaluation (Tyler 1950). Dressel's 21 "general principles of curriculum construction" examine the curriculum from many positions (see Mayhew and Ford 1971 for a summary).

In the best tradition of American pragmatism is the "competency-based" approach to curriculum. A product of the last 20 years, it has been fully articulated in the experience of Alverno College. But stated "competence" is also characteristic of programs that lead to external certification or licensing, such as nursing, business, and engineering. The same goal-oriented approach to the curriculum is found in the contemporary emphasis on "outcomes" (Pascarella and Terenzini 1991; see also Bergquist, Gould, and Greenberg 1981 for a comprehensive inventory of outcomes and a matrix for assessment, and McKelvie 1986 and Pazandak 1989 for a discussion of the value of goals in a large university setting).

In looking for guidance to develop a working definition of the curriculum, one caveat is worth noting. At an early meeting of any committee, study group, or task force, someone will likely recommend that a comprehensive statement of philosophy must precede any detailed consideration. Philosophy in education is tricky business. At the start of a project, philosophical assumptions have to be made, but they are not *the* philosophy. The full meaning, the "philosophy of the curriculum," cannot be known until the working components are in place and the program has been operating for a time.

> *The history of the curriculum is one in which theories are never realized in the manner they are intended. There are always unintended, unanticipated, and unwilled consequences as theories are put into social action* (Popkewitz 1988, p. 69).

Many a curriculum committee has foundered because at the first meeting—and every one thereafter—someone insisted that the philosophy be fully articulated before any action be undertaken.

The Design Approach

Reviews of curricular projects, successful and unsuccessful, observation of curriculum committees and task forces wrestling with issues of the curriculum, and an examination of proposals for overhauling undergraduate studies stimulate an interesting proposition. Effective organizing principles for the curriculum are likely to be found at a lower level of abstraction than "theory," "philosophy," or "historical dialectic." The concept of design is just such a principle. It is supported by a sound conceptual framework that is less demanding than a fully formulated theory but easily overcomes the sins of instrumentalism. The heart of this approach is to deal with the curricular sector of practice as a *problem in design.*

Once a "problem" in the realm of practice is defined, all the mature professions have orderly "tools" or artifacts to deal with it. The artifact of the academy is the curriculum.

The notion of artifacts as the means of meeting problems in design is well developed, leading us to see each program of education as an "artifact," an artificial system intended to fulfill a purpose (Simon 1969).

The heart of this approach is to deal with the curricular sector of practice as a problem in design.

Fulfillment of purpose or adaptation to a goal involves a relation among three terms: the purpose or goal, the character of the artifact, and the environment in which the artifact performs. . . . An artifact can be thought of as a meeting point, an "interface" in today's terms, between an "inner" environment, the substance and organization of the artifact itself, and an "outer" environment, the surroundings in which it operates. If the inner environment is appropriate to the outer environment, or vice versa, the artifact will serve its intended purpose (Simon 1969, p. 6).

A fundamental distinction here lies between "artificial systems" and the "natural systems" of science, which aim at understanding, systematic understanding, and prediction with respect to phenomena that already exist in nature.

The artificial world is centered precisely on this interface between the inner and outer environments; it is concerned with attaining goals by adapting the former to the latter. The proper study of those who are concerned with the artificial is the way in which that adaptation of means to environments is brought about, and central to that is the process of design itself.

Historically and traditionally, it has been the task of the science disciplines to teach about natural things: how they are and how they work. It has been the task of engineering schools to teach about artificial things: how to make artifacts that have the desired properties and how to design.

Engineers are not the only professional designers. Everyone designs who devises courses of action aimed at changing existing situations into preferred ones. The intellectual activity that produces material artifacts is no different fundamentally from the one that prescribes remedies for a sick patient or the one that devises a new sales plan for a company or a social welfare policy for a state. Design, so construed, is the core of all professional training; *it is the principal mark that distinguishes the professions from the sciences. Schools of engineering, as well as schools of architecture, business, education, law, and medicine, are all centrally concerned with the process of design* (Simon 1969, p. 55, emphasis added).

In light of this conceptualization, revisions to the curriculum, which seem endless to faculty, and the shades of difference that arise among academic programs are not symptoms of confusion, but evidence of vitality.

What process is postulated by the notion of design? In its usual format, design defines a "problem" and formulates a solution. That solution can never be perfect, only "satisficing" (to use Simon's term)—exactly the case with a curriculum. It is from artists, architects, and engineers that the details emerge. The designer operates with few preconceptions and uses available resources, taking full account of their strengths and shortcomings. The title of a book, *Design. The Problem Comes First* (Bernsen 1982), explicates the pattern. A group of art students offer these defining phrases: "Design is the placing of subject matter so as to put it to its greatest advantage or to have it in the most interesting shape, form, or position possible" (Emerson 1957).

In more esoteric phrases, "a universal process of ordering, evidenced in both the 'physical' and 'mental' spheres, is opening after years of concern with, not beauty, humility, or poetry, but with ELEMENTALS. . . . An epoch of ORDER is opening" (Lancelot Law Whyte, cited in Banham 1974). The "order" that stands at the center of the concept is not casual. "A good design never comes by chance; it is the product of trained intelligence. . . . By design we mean the creating of relationships . . . " (Whyte, cited in Banham 1974).

One great asset of the concept of design is its comprehensive neutrality. The curriculum "designer" is free of presumptions, free to examine components on their relative merits; large classes or small, interdisciplinarity or multidisciplinarity, master classes or studio classes—their value is determined by the place in the design. With an approach involving design, questions are moved to a lower level of abstraction, and, consequently, more dimensions of operation can be considered.

This advantage was first observed nearly a century ago: "When we approach the study of design, from whatever point of view, . . . we can hardly fail to be impressed with [the] vast variety and endless complexity of forms . . . the term covers. . . . The range is enormous" (Crane 1977, p. 1). The essential process in the application of design involves "inventing things [that] display new physical order, organization, form, in response to function" (Alexander 1964, p. 1).

To approach change in the curriculum as a problem in design, not philosophy or technique, fixes the responsibility with the inventor—that is, the faculty. Curriculum as design emphasizes invention, intention, and construction.

> *The essence of the natural sciences is the discovery of hidden patterns or partially concealed ones* [echoes of developmental psychology!]. *Natural phenomena have an air of "necessity" about them. Artificial phenomena have an air of "contingency" in their malleability by the environment* (Simon 1969, p. 3, emphasis added).

It is not surprising that many educational thinkers and writers have touched the edge of the idea of design, for "curriculum theory is about *mix*" (Broudy 1977) and the curriculum is a "social artifact" (Rudolph 1977). "Theory is inadequate to the tasks of the curriculum" (Schwab 1969).

A Framework for Design Analysis

If "design" holds advantages over "theory" as the means of investing the curriculum with practical effectiveness, how can it be applied? Any elaboration of the idea should give boundaries and reasonable specificity, but, most important, the refinement of definitions should not go to such detail that it hampers the judgment of those who have to work with it.

The implications of the preceding subsection can be woven into a comprehensive definition: *The curriculum is an intentional design for learning negotiated by faculty in light of their specialized knowledge and in the context of social expectations and students' needs.* That definition might be a bit stodgy, but it does sharpen the point that a curriculum is an artifact produced by a particular faculty for students at a particular institution. The essential qualities are all there: faculty responsibility, specialized knowledge, intended outcomes, negotiated relationships, and a learning plan for students.

The components of design as they apply to higher education must be identified. Readily adaptable from art, engineering, and science are the three basic components of design—context, content, and form (see figure 1)—and each component can be elaborated to fit higher education. The figure provides an open matrix into which most curricular change can be fitted. Probably the simplest application of these components is as a checklist to describe fully what is contained and implied in a given academic program. The open matrix is also useful for comparing the features of one unit of the curriculum to another. It can function as a planning format that presents current versus intended states. It can aid an evaluation of practice against ideal or intended features. And the order of the major components, context, content, and form, can be rearranged to reflect priorities. For example, form might be elevated to a primary position if the "design problem" focuses on a comprehensive introduction of computer technology across the curriculum.

What such an analytical schema ensures is a complete beginning, not a solution. It has been used in research on curricula dealing with environmental studies programs (Molinari 1982), professional preparation of athletic trainers (Wentzel 1986), and institutional comparisons (Li Bao Ming 1991). Faculty groups in several settings, among them nursing, continuing education, and general education, have adapted it.

A Working Terminology
If the first challenge of curriculum is defining the concept, the second is adding a systematic terminology that will set out workable segments. Once a curricular issue is seen as a "problem in design," the next questions are, "What do we look at? How does one designate the scope and dimension of the problem?" The answers determine the nature of resources to be invested. The terminology proposed in this subsection is based on operational scope and the level of faculty members' engagement.

In the normal scheme of things, faculty members' attention day by day is fully occupied with keeping up to date in their fields, holding courses on track, and planning classes. Again and again, faculty report that keeping up with their field is *the* major function (Bowen and Schuster 1986, p. 283). In surveys, interviews, and self-reports, faculty show little appreciation for other aspects of the curriculum.

Ordinarily, much of the curriculum operates as a tacit design, accepted but not fully examined. Only intermittently

FIGURE 1

COMPONENTS OF CURRICULUM DESIGN:
An Open Matrix

1. CONTEXT

Examples

● **Social and Cultural Influences**

• How society defines the functions of higher education; expectations

    • Cultivate expert work force, build responsible citizens, sustain elite leadership, provide upward mobility

• Filtering and interpretive influences

    • Prevailing cultural waves (free speech in the 1960s, "me-ism" in the 1980s, issues of equity)

    • Political, social, economic events: wars, depressions, civil rights movement

    • Pressures of a "hidden curriculum"

● **Direct Influences, Environmental Factors**

• Legislation, public policy

    • G.I. Bill, NDEA, student loan programs, draft exemptions, civil rights decisions in courts

• Market forces, labor markets, financial markets

    • Placement patterns, interest rates

• Demographic trends and events

    • Baby boom, immigration, sex ratio, single-parent homes

• Value of knowledge-in-use, technology-in-demand

    • Post-*Sputnik* emphasis on science, business boom of the 1980s

● **Organizational/Institutional Climate**

• Institutional features

    • Tradition, "saga," culture, administrative structure, faculty ethos

    • Student cultures and subcultures

    • Ecology of service area

• Community dimensions

2. CONTENT

● **Nature of Significant Knowledge:**
  Epistemology

• Structure of organized knowledge

    • Principles, theories, laws, bodies of information

• Methods of establishing and verifying knowledge

    • Styles of inquiry, systems of proof, technique

FIGURE 1 (continued)

- Subsets of related knowledge

- "Ideal-typical" role

- Prerequisite and conjunctive disciplines and fields
- Expected role attributes, "knowledge-in-action" behaviors

- **Nature of Learning: Psychology of Field**
- Learning strategies for apprehending the field at higher cognitive levels
- Students' capacities and learning styles; preconditions of maturity, experience, schooling

- Laboratory, clinical, field experience
- Perfect pitch for music, physical vigor and coordination, aptitude for spatial relations, work experience

- **Affective Domain: Values, Attitudes, Beliefs**
- Helpful personality traits, orienting values, attitudes, beliefs

- Licensed "expertise," orientations toward helping, precision in observations

- **Consequences of Knowledge Holding: Manifest and Latent**
- Cognitive outcomes, "certain knowledge" of field
- Patterns of habit and trained behaviors
- Sensitivities and appreciations
- Components of skill and technique, competencies

3. FORM
- **Distribution of Learning Resources: Time, Space, Facilities**
- Faculty work load

- Contact hours, preparation, course development, advising, in-house, extramural service, research and scholarship
- Inventory of faculty training, survey of interests
- Class/study mix, part-time work, structure of credit

- Faculty expertise: matching talent to learning designs
- Student time distribution, weighting credits

- Budgetary system, allocation methods, priorities, adjustments
- Allocation of physical facilities, space, equipment, services

- **Instructional Strategies and Prevailing Modes of Instruction**
- Calendar and scheduling system; class size, composition, and sorting processes; instructional strategies; alternatives to formal study

- Challenge exams, advanced placement, credit for life experiences, tutorials, projects

FIGURE 1 (continued)

• Integrating learning experiences, applications of knowledge

• Study abroad, honors programs, senior seminars, case studies, internships, voluntary service, field study

● **Proximate Outcomes and Assessments**

• Standardized tests of formal knowledge, external examiners, competency reviews

• GRE, LSAT, MCAT, ACT—Comp; licensing, certification, and accrediting boards; performance portfolios, evaluations of specific skills

• Qualitative assessments

• Student self-reports, situational measures, involvement summaries

• Career development and entry experience, formal grading and reporting procedures

• Alumni surveys, feedback from employers, placement data, policies on grades, transcripts, privacy

do academics take the measure of the curriculum, and then only a few at a time (Stark et al. 1988, p. 88). "There is often little collective work on the curriculum. Rather, courses 'belong' to a professor who exercises exclusive control over their content. Thus, in the extreme, hiring decisions determine the curriculum" (K.S. Louis, cited in Pazandak 1989, p. 18).

But the "course" and the "curriculum" are real entities. "Social facts are things," and in this case both course and curriculum are discrete entities. "If you wish to witness instant shock, ask a faculty member to talk about the curriculum. . . . Yet the curriculum lies at the heart of education. . . . Its grand design is a matter of the greatest consequence" (Enarson 1987).

Two lines of systematic search and invention mark the effort to get beyond a fixation with courses into a terminology that reflects the wider reach of learning. One is taxonomic, the other functional.

Taxonomic approaches are the most popular. They mirror the process of the natural sciences, examining, describing, sometimes measuring, and sorting according to prominent characteristics cases in the field. These features are then laid out in a hierarchy of family, genus, species, and variety.

A field-based inventory (Levine 1981) stops short of the Carnegie Foundation's full classification. While eight common prototypes or models (Bergquist and Phillips 1977) encourage comparative study, the technical precision needed for wide application is limited. Three key elements are necessary for the making of a curriculum: content, pedagogy, and social purpose (Marsden 1989).

Functional categories are derived from concepts or premises held to be critical to the processes of teaching, learning, or development.

An interesting and enlightening common-sense approach uses "course structure, course content, teaching methods, assessment, and industrial experience" to compare the curriculum in chemistry in the Grandes Ecoles of France with British universities (Sutcliffe 1982, p. 57). The comparisons clearly describe the differences and open the way to fruitful consideration of the pros and cons of each.

A functional terminology of "six curricular dimensions"— time, space, resources, organization, procedures, and outcomes—can be used to describe a college curriculum in terms of a series of decisions that the college has made with reference to each of these six dimensions (Bergquist, Gould, and Greenberg 1981, p. 5). In an interesting application of what might be called "reverse English," respondents are presented with 57 statements in a "curriculum orientation profile" with which they can "agree" or "disagree" (Babin 1979, p. 38). The statements are scored according to five categories based on the purpose of education, development of cognitive processes, curriculum as technology, self-actualization, social reconstruction or relevance, and academic rationalism, all abstracted from the literature. Another approach to the problem of terminology postulates a paradigmatic structure to the curriculum (Chickering et al. 1977). Others emphasize the decision-making qualities reflected by the curriculum, citing the systemic, interactive, and nonlinear attributes of those decisions (Conrad and Pratt 1983), or emphasize the division of authority and apply the distinctions to various functions (Tellefsen 1990).

Each of these approaches has virtues in helping to understand and describe the complexity of the curriculum. They do not, however, always make a connection with the curriculum as faculty members encounter it day by day. The "design for learning" formulation (Stark and Lowther 1986, p. 7), with its concentric domains arrayed around curricular functions, goes a long way toward spanning that gap. The gap to practice is closed, perhaps foreclosed, with a tightly knit set of design procedures based on instructional development (Diamond 1989).

A terminology that combines the emphasis on design with dimensions close to the realities of practice could be even more useful. The value of such a typology resides in its capacity to establish a focus or scope to curricular change. When they are confronted with large or pressing issues, people have a tendency to exaggerate the scope to gain emphasis. It is neither necessary nor desirable to mobilize an entire institution around changes in the curriculum to address, for example, quantitative reasoning. A key point in this monograph is that clear definitions of scope and intentions lie at the heart of effective curricular change.

The terminology developed in the rest of this section takes account of the operating components of the curriculum at five levels: course, pattern, constellation, program, and curriculum (see figure 2). Three of these terms—course, program, and curriculum—are entirely familiar, although the refinement of their meaning might be new. The other two are derived from understanding and use that have gone unlabeled, even though teaching faculty often acknowledge them in discussions. Their potential for analytical use is suggested as several critical aspects of each term are pointed out: The nature of the unit is specified; primary interest groups, stake holders, and actors identified; some major kinds and sources of information noted; and possible mediums of action and modalities of professional practice discussed.

Courses
Faculty view their courses as the fundamental unit of practice in the teaching-learning domain and the basic building block of the curriculum. The unit is a nearly universal phenomenon bonded to the nature of the discipline (Clark 1987, p. 184), and courses have exhibited their durability throughout history.

As a basic device, the course is probably the most durable element in American higher education. Entities . . . recognizable as courses already dominated the curriculums of traditional American colleges in the mid-19th century, though they were not so often of equivalent intensity or duration, and their extremely small number made it possible to describe them with much less formality. . . . The course and grade survived with so little challenge for reasons that

FIGURE 2

A TERMINOLOGY FOR CURRICULUM ANALYSIS

Course
What: Basic building block of a curriculum and fundamental unit of professional practice for academics. Can be subdivided into modules or units.

Who: The domain of individual faculty members. Students' role is reactive. Departmental interest is usually tacit.

How: Course reviews best conducted by three-person team from within the department, concentrating on description.

Pattern
What: Groups of courses related by internal affinities of knowledge, technique, or methodology. Commonality of content in such sets of courses the hallmark.

Who: Faculty members from involved departments plus department heads. Deans hold role of observer/monitor.

How: Interdepartmental committees review plans and practice for coherence and redundancy.

Constellation
What: Courses related by common goals or objectives, oriented toward similar outcomes.

Who: Deans and/or program directors hold the initiative. Faculty in committees or task forces make decisions. Chief academic officer has supporting role. Aims must be clear to students.

How: Standing committees or commissions have oversight. Specialized staff support might be needed.

Program
What: An arrangement of courses and learning options that leads to publicly recognized certificates or credentials.

Who: Deans hold a primary interest. External bodies, usually professional associations or licensing boards, participate.

How: External reviews play a major role. Consultants, advisory committees, and self-studies are significant.

Curriculum
What: An institution's entire educational program.

Who: Chief academic officer in charge or initiatives. Deans and faculty responsible for operations. Board of trustees has oversight. State could have a formal responsibility.

How: Comprehensive, process-oriented academic plan requiring various working papers and position documents.

*were no doubt as much psychological as they were histor-
ical. Both were primarily instruments of control* (Veysey
1973, p. 62).

It is at the level of course that the greatest sense of responsibility and commitment to the discipline resides. Few would
question the importance held by courses in U.S. education.
The difficulty arises when it is necessary to consider other
levels of learning.

*The way in which a discipline structures its knowledge
provides the best structure for transmitting it to students
[is one untenable assumption]. . . . The distinction I wish
to make here is between what can be called the logical and
epistemological arrangement of subject matter, on the
one hand, and the "learning structure" on the other* (Glaser 1968).

**Students
exercise their
interests
largely
through "veto
power"—the
capacity to
reject a given
course.**

The stake holders and actors are individual faculty members
with students as implicated bystanders. The province of individual faculty members' control over courses has the qualities
of a sacred right. To address any curricular issue, however,
ways must be found to factor in the external implications of
a course as well as its intrinsic qualities. Students exercise
their interests largely through "veto power"—the capacity to
reject a given course.

Sources of information for the construction or review of
a given course begin with the relationship between the structure of the discipline and the syllabus of the course, then
move to more complex relationships. Fortunately, the last
10 years have been marked by widespread attention within
the disciplines—chemistry, sociology, and history have been
the leaders—to the material to be taught and the method.

From experience with change in curriculum at Wellesley
College come the kind of questions that reach across disciplinary courses and broaden the span of concern: "What are
the *shaping dimensions* (content, scope, methodolgy) of the
discipline at present? How would the discipline need to
change to reflect the fact that women are half the world's pop-
ulation and have had, in one sense, half the world's experience?" (McIntosh 1983, p. 2).

A second kind of information about courses deals with what
might be termed "presentation," these days a bit more pal-

atable than "pedagogy." The concentration is on the appropriateness of relations between the material and the learner, the "learning structure." Often it is easier to stimulate course analysis by opening the prospects of new techniques than to start with content or elusive goals. Workshops or seminars in a nonprescriptive mode that illustrate a variety of techniques, such as team teaching (LaFauci 1970), collaborative learning, computer-assisted learning, and experiential learning, offer a nonthreatening introduction to review of a course (Harris 1987). In recent years, more and more institutions provide special support—release time, grants, summer supplements—to develop courses.

One modality for improvement in this sector of the curriculum is course review. The scrutiny of courses is usually left to the faculty member and no one else. More useful is a departmental review by three-person teams that examine syllabi, texts, classroom techniques, and evaluation. If the courses taught by the teams' members are interrelated, the way is opened to examine relationships among courses. The emphasis is on description, not justification. Because the intellectual harmonics of each course echo across related studies, reviews by collegial teams tend to be very useful. At the outset, participants deserve to be reminded that they are their own experts: In the setting of a college or university, no band of curriculum "experts" is waiting in the wings whose knowledge is demonstrably superior to that of the faculty.

Patterns

Arrangements of related courses constitute the next functional level. The term "patterns" is not in general use, but the idea, groups of courses that are related to each other by virtue of internal affinities of knowledge, skills, and methodolgy, is readily recognized. Interdependence among courses, a commonality of substance, has long been recognized informally, but systematic attention to the implications of relationships has seldom been explored. Three basic structures are possible: sequential, associative, and parallel. Only the first is used with any regularity. Relationships between courses lie at the heart of analyzing a curriculum.

In the natural sciences, strings of prerequisites are the means to expanding, in steps, the understandings students have of the discipline. Other fields have emulated the sequential pattern, often as a matter of convenient scheduling. In an associative pattern, courses are related in a kind of mosaic: It does not matter which is taken first so long as the whole area is covered. Many student-designed programs have an underlying expectation that an associative pattern will be the final outcome. The assumption is also apparent in fields like literature or history.

The notion of parallel relationships is less developed, although the idea was applied with good results in the cultural studies introduced under the sponsorship of the National Defense Education Act of the 1960s. The idea is that students who study, say, 19th century European history will gain from a tacit exchange of ideas if they pursue courses in Victorian prose and poetry and the Romantic Movement in German literature at the same time.

The actors and stake holders in pattern analysis are faculty within the disciplinary departments and in closely related fields, often those sharing in preparation for professional cer-tification. Students' interests are largely inferred rather than solicited, with the final judgement left to reaction and response.

Currently, several strong lines of interest are best addressed through pattern analysis; writing-across-the-curriculum is prominent among them. The more successful approaches overreach departments (McLeod 1988; White 1989). The place of computers in the curriculum can be analyzed at this level, although widespread variation and some confusion about how to deal with this technology still exist (Cohen 1983; Haigh 1985). Critical thinking is another phenomenon that cuts across courses that benefits from pattern analysis (Meyers 1986). Interest is rising rapidly in scientific and technical understanding, again, as it interacts across courses (Brun-schwig and Breslin 1982). Options for creative study that link business and languages as preparation for international mar-keting or management and packages joining statistics and research methodolgy reflect such thinking. Still other topics that can benefit from pattern analysis are clusters focusing on civic responsibility, leadership, and professional ethics.

A modality for working through these curricular issues is an interdepartmental committee, study group, or task force. The scope of the charge can be made very specific, and bene-ficial outcomes are usually clear: less repetition of material, more varied perspectives on the same phenomenon, supple-mentary views, or consolidated common insights.

Especially appropriate for dealing with patterns of courses and all the higher levels of analysis of the curriculum is a "two-committee structure," separating the exploratory, information-gathering stage from the decision stage. The first committee is charged with surrounding the issue, bringing views forward, and developing alternatives, not decisions. The second committee is charged with recommending a decision and action plan.

Constellations

Another level of focus is those clusters of courses with a distinct shape or form. Again, the term is not generally used, but the idea is well understood. "Constellations" are groups of courses related to one another by their mode of response to some *common aim,* a commonality of goals, to extrinsic factors rather than intrinsic relationships in the subject matter. Often that aim has a rationale of its own and must be clearly communicated. Major and minor course sets and the general education sector are the prominent examples. It is the proposals for new constellations, however, that today present the most interesting challenges to the curriculum: women's studies; African-American studies; non-Western civilization; emphases on ethnicity and diversity; global studies; science, technology, and society; and so on. A critical issue, as discussed later, is whether these topics affect the entire curriculum or just one sector.

The interest groups, stake holders, and actors at this level cover a much wider range than for a course or pattern. Students' interest is frequently direct and vocal. Frequently, interest groups external to the university have a stake in the outcome and the process. Even though faculty are the source of information and judgment, only the top administration can command and orchestrate the use of the resources likely to be required for a thorough analysis of a constellation. The chief academic officer, the provost, or a vice president necessarily plays a major role as the convening authority—although not necessarily the sponsor.

Sources of information on the topics arising here are likely to be rich and varied. Staff support will probably be required to collect, organize, and distribute materials. Time is a major factor: As much as two academic years might be required for study, communication, and negotiation. At this level, the costs of analyzing the curriculum and the recurring future costs of change rise substantially and can rarely be absorbed into normal operating expenditures. Only a major task force or commission planning for operations over several years is likely to give complete results. Investment in the process itself becomes a matter of prime importance.

Programs

Collections of courses that lead to certification or credentials lie at the heart of institutional accountability, and the complexities are familiar territory to anyone who has participated in regional or professional accreditation. Among the essential features of "programs," as the term is used in this monograph, is the requirement for communicability. The public expects that persons certified through an educational program will hold and act on certain knowledge, skills, and understandings.

The stake holders, interest groups, and actors for programs are extended by one more degree. External parties like licensing boards, advisory bodies, visiting evaluators, professional societies, and even state legislatures are always involved at this level of curricular analysis. The dean holds much of the initiative. The form and substance of review at this level are often prescribed, what has been called the "outside-in syndrome" (Ferguson 1981) or, at the very least, must be respected.

A wide range of possibilities exist for program review, and each exercise is tailored to fit the requirements. Not too many years ago, internal program reviews gained wide attention, largely as an instrument of retrenchment. After one or two experiences, most institutions found the process prohibitively time-consuming, costly, and indeterminate. Because the elements of self-study and iteration that go into program reviews are so costly, they are best reserved for evaluations where the materials can be turned to several uses.

The curriculum

In this suggested terminology, the term "curriculum" is reserved for an institution's entire educational program. It is the locus of corporate responsibility for learning that engages faculty, trustees, administration, and students. The curriculum encompasses all the sectors of the institution involved with the process of teaching and learning.

Issues appropriate for addressing at this level are very few, but they are among the most important for an institution's future—for example, what profile of programs best fits the institution. Issues must be selected and treated with care. It is both a tactical and strategic error to declare an issue to be a problem of the curriculum if it really lies with a program or constellation.

Leadership among the actors and stake holders resides with the senior academic officer, provost, or academic vice president. The president's and the trustees' major functions are oversight and support. All of the faculty have a primary stake in the character of the curriculum. Issues that are truly curricular in scope will affect all courses in some way, for the most critical decisions determine the learning environment, define the conditions of professional practice, and change the financial operations of a college, school, or university.

A full review of the curriculum opens so many demands for information that it can seldom be undertaken without a special staff unit charged with coordinating responsibility. As subsequent sections point out, the self-study has become the instrument of choice. Costs are high, and presidents often seek outside funding from friends of the institution or foundations. The amount of time required is also large, taking as much as three or four years to reach implementation.

— 0 —

No segment of academic programs has escaped scrutiny and criticism over the last six years. The next section examines impacts of and reactions to curricular change.

FORCES OF CHANGE: Critics, Curricular Reforms, Crossroads, and Practices

The dearth of a literature on systematic approaches to the design and evaluation of higher education curricula is not accidental. It reflects not only the invisible, elusive, and political nature of the design and evaluation process, but [also] the status of the higher education curriculum itself (Wood and Davis 1978, p. 6).

In the years since 1978, analyses about how higher education's curriculum should be designed and evaluated have proliferated. The explosion has come primarily from three different angles: (1) national reports about the curriculum and a concern for quality; (2) critical explorations about the nature of knowledge; and (3) specific examples of colleges and universities that have undertaken curricular experiments.

National Reports of the 1980s: Critics of the Curriculum
The problems
Future historians of U.S. higher education will surely remember the 1980s for the avalanche of reports about postsecondary education that called for dramatic curricular change in undergraduate education (see, e.g., Association of American Colleges [AAC] 1986; Bennett 1984; Boyer and Levine 1981; Mortimer 1984; National Governors Association 1986; Newman 1985; Rudolph 1984). A multitude of well-publicized books and articles criticized different aspects of the curricular experience and called for a multitude of changes in the academic curriculum (Bok 1986; Boyer 1987; Finn 1982). The reports addressed three major questions about the curriculum:

1. How much of the curriculum should be prescribed, and how much should be left to students' choice?
2. What is the best way to achieve breadth in a student's education?
3. How does one teach students to synthesize what they have learned? (Bok 1986).

The Closing of the American Mind (Bloom 1987) attempted to answer these queries using the language of polemic. Bloom believed that the United States was no longer effective at teaching its young, that its competitive edge had been lost,

---

that what it meant to be liberally educated had evaporated, and that the curriculum had become an incoherent amalgamation of political compromises by faculty and administrators alike. In effect, academe was no longer effective at its central mission—educating and socializing the young.

Many of the national reports agreed with this analysis, albeit in a language and style less inflammatory. The most salient message from the reports was the need to enhance the meaning and quality of the undergraduate curriculum. Incremental change at the edge of the curriculum was no longer enough. Instead, several reports called for an overhaul of the "curricular experience" for undergraduates. According to the reports, a strong liberal arts or general education component must form the core of the undergraduate curriculum. Two reports strongly advocated a prescribed liberal arts core (Association of American Colleges 1986; Bennett 1984). The other reports, although less prescriptive, called for a curriculum that enhances a student's analytical and problem-solving skills. Emphasis within a discipline was encouraged only after a student achieves strong skills in communication and a grounding in a curriculum based on liberal or general education. Many of the reports called for the development of a common core based on classic works that concerned the verities of Western civilization.

In general, the reports also linked co-curricular activities, such as faculty interaction with students and advising, as part of the problems that pervaded academe and demanded attention. For example, the reports emphasized that good teaching must be expected, supported, and rewarded and that attention must be shifted away from research to teaching; senior faculty were encouraged to become more centrally involved with undergraduates through teaching and advising.

The writers of the reports argued that the key to understanding whether an institution's curriculum is successful is through extensive evaluations and assessments. They encouraged a comprehensive evaluation of undergraduate students and of the institution and its faculty to determine whether college programs enabled students to become well-educated, civic-minded graduates with skills that could be used in the marketplace. Calls for institutional effectiveness increased, and assessment of students became a central concern. Of consequence, researchers undertook analyses of course planning and the teaching environment (Stark et al. 1988).

Involvement in Learning (Mortimer 1984) and *College: The Undergraduate Experience* (Boyer 1987) recommended a final, comprehensive evaluation of students that would demonstrate an integration of classroom knowledge with an awareness and valuing of the larger community and society. College programs also were to be evaluated to see whether they were fulfilling their missions and providing a good learning environment for students. Students as well as external agencies needed to be involved in evaluating colleges and programs.

Finally, many of the reports emphasized that curricular excellence should be defined in relation to an institution's mission. Simply stated, if the participants in academe did not know what they were trying to accomplish, how would they know whether they were accomplishing it? In particular, "there is so much confusion as to the mission of the American college and university that it is no longer possible to be sure why a student should take a particular program of courses" (Association of American Colleges 1986, p. 2).

The causes

According to the reports, the situation in which higher education found itself could be traced to:

1. The reforms made in the 1960s;
2. The fundamental problems generated by declining resources in the 1970s and 1980s; and
3. The changed perceptions of key constituencies in higher education about the purpose of higher education and thus the curriculum.

A supporter of the revisionist views of the 1960s noted:

The late sixties and early seventies were the darkest hours in the history of American higher education, a dark night of the institutional soul from which we have not yet and may not ever fully recover. In their disdain for standards and their demand for relevance, our cultural continuity was eroded and any institutional sense of morality regarding a student's course work, conversation, conduct, or sexual conquest was obliterated. . . . Now, in the eighties, we are trying to pick up the pieces (Holland 1985, p. 58).

This lament was widespread. Summing up the cause of academe's curricular problems succinctly, Saul Bellow wrote,

"The university has become inundated and saturated with the backflow of society's problems" (in Bloom 1987, p. 18). Clearly, the "backflow" referred to previously underrepresented constituencies in academe, among them minorities and women. It is these people, the argument goes, whose demands for relevance caused the curriculum to become watered down and saturated with trivial texts at the expense of the classical curriculum.

Thus, the quality of the curriculum was placed in opposition to educational access.

As laudable as it may be as an ideal, the widening of access also has contributed to the confusions that have beset the baccalaureate experience. The tension between democratic values and the effort to maintain standards for an undergraduate education can be creative, but too often numbers and political considerations have prevailed over quality (Association of American Colleges 1986, p. 5).

Further:

The issue of access has dominated higher education since the 1960s. Quality became a secondary concern, in part because the early covenant did not specify standards for the programs to which access should be provided. . . . As a way of extending access to all levels of higher education, faculty and administrators lowered standards for courses, student promotion, and graduation (Conrad 1985a, p. 2).

An additional cause of the demise of the curriculum was traced to students who had become consumers where the labor market dominated what they would take. The proliferation of professional and technical courses and the concomitant decline in the humanities and social sciences could be traced to heightened job requirements where knowledge for knowledge's sake was no longer sufficient. The catchword of the 1960s—relevance—remained important, but instead of a curriculum that was relevant to understanding society's problems, students sought courses that were relevant to the marketplace.

The reports often criticized faculty and administrators for failing to enhance the meaning and quality of the undergraduate curriculum. Inadequate presidential authority over internal affairs and lack of faculty leadership in curricular matters received a special amount of criticism. "The decline was caused in part by a failure of nerve and faith on the part of many college faculties and administrators, and persists because of a vacuum in educational leadership" (Bennett 1984, p. 2).

Faculty were recognized as central to the process of changing the curriculum: They are the professional staff charged with designing and delivering undergraduate instruction. Yet, according to the reports, they had neglected their duties: "Central to the troubles and to the solutions are the professors" (Association of American Colleges 1986, p. 6). "The American faculty has generally been a reprehensible failure" (Muscatine 1985, p. 18).

Similarly, academic administrators were charged with initiating change and bringing faculty together toward a common purpose, but, the reports suggested, administrators instead had tended to emphasize off-campus duties and a myopic view of the institution. The president and other principal academic officers were excoriated for abdicating their roles as major actors in formulating curricular missions for their institutions. Throughout the 1980s, presidents increasingly viewed themselves as fundraisers, and academic leaders like academic deans became caught up in the more prosaic day-to-day details that demanded increased time and attention. The reports called for a reassertion of presidential authority and prerogative and a more active role to be played by academic administrators (see, e.g., Kerr and Gade 1987).

Clearly, the "backflow" referred to previously underrepresented constituencies in academe, among them minorities and women.

Responses to the critics

The responses to the reports were almost as voluminous as the reports themselves (Altbach 1987; Lee 1985; Stark and Lowther 1986; Stark et al. 1988). An analysis of the reports and commentaries offered seven questions that pervaded the discussions of curriculum reform:

1. Who is to decide the curriculum of schools and colleges in a democratic society?
2. To what extent should students be involved in planning and developing the curriculum?
3. What are the relative rights and responsibilities of teachers within schools and of society outside schools?
4. What is the meaning of the liberal arts in undergraduate programs?

5. What is the purpose and function of general education?
6. What are the specific benefits and advantages that accrue to the college graduate upon the completion of program and degree requirements?
7. What is the particular significance and meaning that can be attached to a college education in an era of universal education? (Fincher 1986).

Additional authors analyzed the reports and offered harsh opinions about the reports' findings. Different authors believed that discussions about the curriculum had to include a broad range of issues that went well beyond the curriculum. "The real limitation of the reports is their attempt to isolate curriculum and instruction from other problems" (Benjamin 1985, p. 28).

All the reports on education . . . have made the same two mistakes. One, they sought to improve education by focusing on schools themselves, and two, they failed to ask, education for what type of society? (Rossides 1987, p. 426).

This criticism of the reports was that they did not sufficiently focus on how education operates in American society and that they painted education as if it were a nonpolitical activity.

Is the focus on solving problems through an apolitical education not a way to avoid democratically determined solutions? Is the call for research, whether stemming from conservatives or liberals, not a way to pretend that the policies of the powerful are rational, above politics, and value neutral? (Rossides 1987, p. 427).

These questions have roots in the enduring traditions of debates about curriculum in American society and provide the foundation for a discussion about alternative curricular analyses.

A historical perspective
The criticism in the 1980s—although significant for the sheer volume of reports, articles, and books generated—was not new. "The current attempt to unify the humanities curriculum around some vision of educational fundamentals is only the

latest in a long series of such efforts, which have invariably ended in futility" (Gerald Graff [*Chronicle of Higher Education,* 17 February] 1988, p. A48). A review of the history of U.S. higher education reveals how often higher education's curricular offerings and those who manage the curriculum have been criticized.

In 1828, for example, writers argued much the same as Bloom for maintaining the classical curriculum (Conrad 1985b, p. 110). Nicholas Murray Butler in 1905 spoke about the need for "an end of the idling and dawdling that now characterize so much of American higher education" (cited in Rudolph 1977, p. 207). In 1936, Robert Maynard Hutchins wrote, "Unless some such demonstration or some such evangelistic movement can take place, we shall remain in our confusion; we shall have neither general education nor universities; and we shall continue to disappoint the hopes of our people (cited in Rudolph 1977, p. 87). And in 1966, Daniel Bell, in *The Reforming of General Education,* wrote, "It has been suggested that liberal arts education has lost its force . . . that the requirements of early specialization are in the process of transforming the college into a preprofessional school" (cited in Lee 1985). Clearly, the debate about what students should learn—and who should decide what students should learn—has been with academe since its inception; alternative conceptions of the curriculum, however, are currently being developed that reorient the nature of the debate.

Reconceptualizations: Curricular Debate at a Crossroads

Twenty years ago, the two principal alternative critiques of the curriculum were *Pedagogy of the Oppressed* (Freire 1970) and *Deschooling Society* (Illich 1971), both of which used a Marxist perspective in their analyses. Subsequently, Marxist scholars concerned with political economy also have argued that the curriculum in complex societies reproduces the class inequalities that occur in the larger society, that the curriculum maintains inequality among classes by teaching working class students one set of skills and upper class students another (Bowles and Gintis 1976).

Based on investigations into the curriculum from a multitude of other perspectives (see, e.g., Berstein 1977; Bourdieu and Passeron 1977; Giroux 1983; Graff [*Chronicle,* 17 February] 1988; Grumet 1983; Schubert 1986; Tierney 1989a), however, we can no longer assume that an alternative conceptualization of the curriculum is based solely on Marxist theory. Such diverse arenas as the sociology of knowledge, literary theory, the philosophy of science, and postmodernism often stand in sharp contrast to one another. What the proponents of the alternative conceptualization share is the rejection of the idea that a common canon of knowledge exists that should be transmitted to all students. Although the language and theoretical constructs the alternative theorists call upon are abstract and often difficult to conceptualize, their arguments about the curriculum recently have raised a considerable amount of discussion in the higher education community. The alternative theorists ask several central questions about the curriculum:

1. How is knowledge reproduced?
2. What are the sources of knowledge students acquire?
3. How do students and teachers resist or contest what is conveyed through lived experiences in schools?
4. What impact does the curriculum have on students' outlook?
5. Whose interests are served by the outlooks fostered in the curriculum?
6. When served, do these interests move more in the direction of emancipation, equity, and social justice, or in the opposite direction?
7. How can students be empowered through the curriculum? (Schubert 1986).

These questions challenge the fundamental assumptions upon which traditional curricular theory has been based, in the process rejecting many of the conclusions of the earlier reports. For example, in opposition to Bloom's assumption that a common body of knowledge exists to which all students should be introduced, the alternative theorists conceive of knowledge as a set of discourses governed by ideological conflicts of class, race, and gender. Consequently, the manner in which knowledge is defined and structured by way of academic departments and disciplines has been brought into question (Schuster and Van Dyne 1984; Weaver 1981). The point is not to do away with all disciplinary boundaries but to delineate how knowledge is conceptualized so that teachers and students understand the ideological and cultural constraints surrounding the curriculum. The theorists' assumption is that how an institution arranges components of the curriculum commits the institution to philosophical and political choices, whether recognized or not.

Thus, the alternative theorists have redefined the curriculum by questioning what counts for knowledge. Like any new approach, different definitions of the curriculum compete for acceptance. One of the most widely accepted is the following:

By curriculum I mean what students have an opportunity to learn in school, through both the hidden and overt curriculum, and what they do not have an opportunity to learn because certain matters were not included in the curriculum, referred to . . . as the "null curriculum" (McCutcheon 1982, p. 19).

Thus, what students have an opportunity to study orients attention on selecting an object of study and how it is presented to the exclusion of other objects (Cherryholmes 1988, p. 133). The purpose of the study of curriculum, then, becomes the discovery of why some pieces of knowledge are taught and others are not. The curriculum becomes an ongoing process of the construction of knowledge in which organizational participants determine what counts as knowledge, what knowledge is worthy of transmitting, and what organizational forms are appropriate (Gumport 1988; Tierney 1989a). Thus, the curriculum is viewed as centrally linked to pedagogy and the culture of the institution in which it occurs.

One of the primary thrusts for this position comes from the explosion of knowledge resulting from recent research on women and minorities. As women and minority scholars investigated their collective pasts, they often found a lack of substantive research; curricular studies also brought to light how women and minorities have been excluded from general education, liberal studies, the sciences, requirements of Western civilization, and the like (Aiken et al. 1987; Schuster and Van Dyne 1985). Feminist studies, in particular, have brought to light the need to transform present curricular structures so that, some would argue, "the use of feminist scholarship to transform existing courses has emerged as a popular academic movement" (Glazer 1987, p. 293).

The undergirding assumption of this approach is that an "invisible paradigm" orients the curriculum in one direction. Women's studies have focused attention on:

. . . the "invisible paradigms" of the academic system and the larger cultural contexts that marginalize or trivialize the lives of all women, the lives of blacks and of ethnic minorities, and those outside the dominant class or culture. Invisible paradigms . . . are the infrastructure of our academic system. For us, the invisible paradigms are the internalized assumptions, the network of unspoken agreements, the implicit contracts that all participants in the process of higher education have agreed to, usually unconsciously, to bring about learning (Schuster and Van Dyne 1985, p. 8).

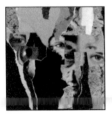

This invisible paradigm means more than unearthing a hidden curriculum. Previously, the concept of a hidden curriculum sought to explain how relatively obvious examples—who was on a reading list and who was not—masked the dominant ethos so that education reproduced the inequities in society. The purpose of understanding a hidden curriculum was to incorporate what had been excluded into a unifying synthesis. The point is not merely to add previously excluded women or minority authors to required courses, however, so that one literary canon becomes substituted for another and consensus is reached. Instead, "the traditional emphasis on consensus is replaced by a focus on conflict, . . . on social structures, and the construction of meaning" (Giroux 1983, p. 56). Invisible paradigms, then, are investigations that seek to understand how ideologies and cultures operate within an organization so that power is defined in a particular way.

Thus, the alternative theorists seek to expose how the existing institutional frameworks guide the curriculum. In this light, changing courses so that minority or women authors are included is relatively insignificant and counterproductive if the dominant structure is reaffirmed by those changes. Students should be exposed to a curriculum where they "not only read the masterpieces of Western culture, but also look at the system of authority, the relations of power, and the procedures of legitimation that underwrite canonical knowledge" (Trimbur 1986, p. 117).

The question becomes not how to legitimate one curricular form as opposed to another, but how to question the underlying structures of knowledge of whatever is taught. Knowledge is no longer something that is an essential truth and transmitted from one generation to the next; rather, knowledge is a social product with political consequences.

> *The student [sees] that his or her understanding of all of culture's texts (from philosophical treatises to popular television shows) is a result of situation in a complex network of gender, class, and race relations and . . . that reason (and meaning) changes depending on whether the reader is a male or female . . . , a Hispanic or white American . . ., [from the] working class or upper class* (Zavarzadeh and Morton 1987, p. 19).

This view also maintains that vast possibilities exist for administrators, faculty, and students to redefine the nature of the learning experience beyond what skills are needed for the work world. In working from the assumption that a curriculum is a powerful act that structures how organizational participants think about and organize knowledge, proponents of this perspective reject the idea that the primary purpose of a curriculum is to inculcate youth with the accumulated wisdom of society. Institutional curricula need to be investigated from the perspective of *whose* knowledge, history, language, and culture are under examination. Conversely, the organization's participants need to uncover those whose voices are not present in a curricular discourse and give life to them (Tierney 1989a).

Like any new conceptualization of a particular problem, one is never sure whether the ideas are durable or merely a fad. One need merely recall concepts from an earlier era, such as management by objectives or the taxonomies of educational objectives (Bloom 1956) to see how fashionable ideas ultimately collapse. The challenges posed by the alternative theorists, however, have placed faculty, administrators, and researchers at an intellectual crossroads. Depending upon the inherent assumptions and values of the organization's participants, an institution's approach to the curriculum can vary widely.

Curricular Practices

In large part, the preponderance of curricular experiments of the 1960s either have been extensively modified or halted. At the same time, a wide variety of curricular changes on campuses have resulted in new forms of academic organization. Dual degree programs, committee-run rather than department-controlled programs of study, and mixed majors, such as language and business, are examples of recent changes that potentially have a far-reaching impact on the structure and function of the academic enterprise. Additionally, calls for dramatic changes in curricular offerings have been cited as necessary for the country to increase its productivity and respond to the needs of industry (Azaroff 1982; Fairweather 1988; Lynton 1981; Lynton and Elman 1987).

Interdisciplinary focus is another change taking hold on countless campuses. The push for interdisciplinary courses and departments comes from two different angles. On the one hand, biotechnology, communications, and materials science are interdisciplinary areas that have resulted from the demands of the external environment. On the other hand, interdisciplinary areas like women's studies, ethnic studies, and literary criticism have been brought about by the research undertaken by the alternative theorists who seek to transcend disciplines to understand the invisible paradigms (Aiken et al. 1987).

A variety of useful texts systematize the curricular changes under way on college campuses, explicating the underlying rationales of different programs of study and offering an understanding of how the theoretical perspectives are enacted (see, e.g., Bergquist and Phillips 1977 for a list of curricular models). A comprehensive taxonomy of curricular undertakings might include:

1. *Heritage based:* A curriculum designed to inculcate students with a knowledge of the past;
2. *Thematic based:* Identificaion and in-depth studies of a specific problem, such as the environment;
3. *Competency based:* The teaching of specific skills, such as proficiency in language and mathematics;
4. *Career based:* Preparation for a specific career;
5. *Experience based:* Opportunities for learning outside the classroom;
6. *Student based:* Providing students with opportunities to control what they learn;
7. *Values based:* Emphasis on specific institutional values;
8. *Future based:* A curriculum concerned with what students will need in the future (Bergquist and Phillips 1977).

Other studies provide helpful overviews to different components of the curriculum (see, e.g., Conrad 1978 for a study of curricular innovation; Conrad and Wyer 1980 and Gaff 1983 for studies of different experiments in the liberal arts; Gamson et al. 1984 for a discussion of liberal education; Levine and Weingart 1973 for an examination of experimentation in 26 schools; and Schuster and Van Dyne 1985 for a series of essays outlining different curricular experiments that focus on integrating women's studies into the curriculum).

Still other studies delineate the difference between telic reforms and popular reforms (Grant and Riesman 1978). Telic reforms are those that "set forth new ideals" and "point toward a different conception of the end of undergraduate education, to distinguish them from the more popular reforms of the last decade [that] have brought about a general loosening of the curriculum" (p. 15). Popular reforms are changes that "modified the means of education within the constraints of the existing goals of the research-oriented university" (p. 16). Two of the more recent and successful telic experiments are on the campuses of Evergreen State College in Olympia, Washington, and Hampshire College in Amherst, Massachusetts (see also Clark 1970). A detailed account of the history of Evergreen State offers ramifications for students, faculty, and administrators of collaborative learning where departments and disciplines do not exist, faculty teach collectively, and the structure of the undergraduate curriculum reflects interdisciplinary coursework (Jones 1981). Similarly, at Hampshire College, the faculty also eschew disciplines and departments, but collaborative learning is not emphasized (Alpert 1980; Patterson and Longworth 1966). Instead, students are viewed as individual learners and the emphasis is on empowering students with the capabilities to become self-sufficient learners. For example, students must develop an idea, recruit a faculty committee, and write a senior thesis as the major part of their senior year. Such a project stands in sharp contrast to the group-oriented activities throughout a student's career at Evergreen State. Nevertheless, both institutions reflect dramatic telic reforms based in large part on alternative conceptualizations of the curriculum.

The question arises then about how one brings about changes in the curriculum. What ingredients, what perspectives, what preparations, and what actions are needed to implement such proposals? The next section considers one possible perspective and then turns to the challenge of preparing for and managing transformation of the curriculum.

THE NATURE OF PROFESSIONAL PRACTICE

Professions

Underpinning the emphasis on application in this monograph is the idea that to be a professor in a college or university is to act in a realm of professional practice analogous to that of the other learned professions—medicine, law, and a range of fields from accounting to the military. All professions, the academic enterprise included, exhibit parallel but not exactly similar attributes (see Cullen 1978). Oddly enough, few professionals want to look at what goes on next door. Academics are no exception, for they exhibit the same tunnel vision, seeing only the special, precious nature of their own field and resisting all intrusion.

All professions, according to traditional sociology, recognize a formal body of knowledge and, increasingly, a set of refined techniques that can be mastered only by long, specialized study. In all professions, expertise is highly differentiated into specialties similar to the disciplines and fields that mark the academy. Within that corpus of expertise, however, is a generic core of knowledge common to all practitioners. These bodies of knowledge and the technique, both core and specialty, are useful and necessary to everyday life. Authorized practitioners therefore put them to practical ends.

Tensions between standard techniques and experimental applications are found across the professions.

Because the body of knowledge, however complex and well-founded it might be, is always tentative and incomplete, such practical applications must be exercised with trained judgment and within the canons of the profession. The risks of having to act, even in the face of incomplete and uncertain knowledge, combined with the responsibility of dealing with clients who are utterly dependent force each profession into a careful definition of "practice." That is to say, each practitioner is bound by circumstances, not always clear, within which he or she is authorized by social convention and discipline of the profession to act, to conduct practice. Each profession has a finite set of practice situations.

Uncertainties of substance and the unrelenting demand for practical action are seldom mentioned when professions are seen only as elite. Today, however, they generate trying dilemmas for every profession. Physicians face the tensions between treatment and prevention. Social workers wrestle with the conflicts of clients' welfare versus society. Collisions between individual practice and institutionalized service are present in fee-based professions. Tensions between standard techniques and experimental applications are found across the professions. Difficulties in reconciling clients' individuality and the field's generalities come up everywhere. It is quite clear that the heart and challenge of every profession, separating professionals from artisans, artists, craftsmen, technicians, and managers, are not the routines of regular practice, however complex they might be, but the serious dilemmas, ambiguities, and paradoxes that surround the main areas of practice.

Professionalization and the Academy

It was largely out of these circumstances, uncertain knowledge and ambiguous practice situations, that the idea of a need for constant "professionalization" came (see Vollmer and Mills 1966). No profession can rest assured on its social status. Recognition of a profession is earned again and again. Every profession must engage constantly in "professionalizing" itself. "To what extent does the occupation possess this attribute and how is it working toward further refinement?" (Houle 1980, p. 27). To constantly professionalize itself, a profession must demonstrate a high degree of self-awareness among practitioners, a strong sense of identity, and constant attention to the state of practice in all its forms.

Conditions in the academic profession that enhance or hamper professionalization are by no means self-evident and need to be examined with candor. Some arise because of differences in structure and conduct, but others come from simple inattention. Put succinctly, the substantive core of the academic profession, knowledge and learning, is well developed: The practice situation is not.

Conditions that enhance academic professionalization rest on the foundations of expertise and the responsibilities that accompany claims to "superior knowledge" (Shils 1983; see also Kadish 1991 for guidelines on establishing within academic institutions the proper setting for ethical judgment). What can also be said with assurance about conditions that enhance professionalization is that the common process of the profession is learning—the learning of practitioners as they strive to keep current in their fields, the learning of researchers generating new knowledge, the learning of students at every level.

We have identified and described four basic functions of faculties—instruction, research, public service, and insti-

*tutional service. [They] are based mostly on a single uni-
fying process, namely, learning. Learning in this sense
means bringing about desired changes in the traits of
human beings (instruction), discovering and interpreting
knowledge (research), applying knowledge to serve the needs
of the general public (public service), and creating an environment that contributes to and facilitates learning (institutional service). Learning is the chief stock in trade of the
professoriate. It occurs in all fields, it takes place in diverse
settings, and it serves varied clienteles* (Bowen and Schuster
1986, p. 23).

In the common practice situation, more than in the bodies
of expertise, the academic community faces the most serious
obstacles to its own professionalization. Some of these limi-
tations come from attitudes of practitioners themselves, others
from indifference toward the dilemmas that surround practice
embedded in an institutional environment. As to the attitu-
dinal factors: No national academic body is available to build
identity and a sense of membership. By any measure, the
American Association of University Professors comes up short
in representing the whole academic profession. Even the most
basic components of practice—academic freedom, for example—have not been encoded or confirmed in the law. No
widely accepted code of ethics exists, and the AAUP Statement
of 1966 is barely a beginning.

Most professions with a history as venerable as the academy
define a minimum level of competence for admission to public practice. Absent such minimum standard or certification,
the academic profession is beset with public criticism and
private doubts, usually around what catches the casual public
eye—the quality of teaching and manifest purposes.

Most professions define a core of generic knowledge common across the domains of practice. Preparation for the academic profession concentrates on specialized knowledge and
leaves the generic component of the process of learning to
the vagaries of on-the-job training and self-education (Bowen
and Schuster 1986, p. 282). Critics past and present have railed
against the indifference toward the locus of common practice,
the teaching-learning situation (Smith 1990). Although some
writers have discussed principles of good practice, in particular consideration of the learner (Chickering and Gamson
1987, p. 3) and construction of productive learning situations,

more than a little confusion exists about whether the core of the profession lies with the discipline or in the broader field of practice.

Without rehearsing the variations on this theme (see Blau 1973; Lieberman 1956; Light 1979; Parsons 1970), one can reach the view that the practice situation is where essential problems of the academic profession reside.

Academic Practice and Its Dilemmas

As noted, academic practice has four domains: instruction, research, public service, and institutional service (Bowen and Schuster 1986). Learning is the process, knowledge the substance, in both instruction and research. Understandably, faculty tend to concentrate on sectors where proprietary interests are strong: instruction in courses and scholarly research. By choice, faculty often entrust the larger dimensions of practice—such as the curriculum—to administrators. In fact, however, the creation and conduct of a sound curriculum call for a high degree of professional collaboration.

The authors' thesis is that the curriculum itself—not courses, teaching, classes, or research—is now a critical element for defining academic practice. Physicians apply their expert knowledge in a practice situation called "treatment"; academics apply their expertise to "learning" situations, a major component of which is the curriculum. Special attention to learning is necessary, and "the way in which a discipline structures its knowledge provides the best structure for transmitting it to students" (Glaser 1968), with a distinction between the "logical and epistemological arrangement of subject matter" and the learning structure. The curriculum is the visible evidence of how faculty interpret theory, application, and values. It is the most public expression of the profession.

The Supreme Court made management of the curriculum a province of faculty practice in the *Yeshiva* decision.

The controlling consideration in this case is that the faculty of Yeshiva University exercise authority which in any other context unquestionably would be managerial. Their authority in academic matters is absolute. They decide what courses will be offered, when they will be scheduled, and to whom they shall be taught. They debate and determine teaching methods, grading policies, and matriculation standards. . . . When one considers the function of a uni-

versity, it is difficult to imagine decisions more managerial than these (National Labor Relations Board v. *Yeshiva University,* 444 U.S. 672 [1980]).

That the design, maintenance, and evaluation of the curriculum are central modalities of professional practice has been asserted by others, but seldom better, since the inauguration speech of Charles William Eliot in 1869:

> *The governing bodies of the University are the Faculties, the Board of Overseers, and the Corporation. The University as a place of study and instruction is, at any moment, what the Faculties make it. The professors, lecturers, and tutors of the University are the living sources of learning and enthusiasm. . . . They personally represent the possibilities of instruction. . . . The discussion of the methods of instruction is the principal business of these bodies. As a fact, progress comes mainly from the Faculties* (Hofstadter and Smith 1961, p. 615).

Responsibility for the curriculum is in no way ambiguous. A joint statement from the American Association of University Professors, the American Council on Education, and the Association of Governing Boards accords the faculty responsibility for curriculum, subject matter and methods of instruction, research, and faculty status as well as the aspects of student life that relate to the educational process. Beyond the management function, the curriculum at any given time is a distillation of knowledge, an epistemological statement, as the faculty see it. It is also the medium of interaction between faculty and students. By every measure of tradition and logic, the curriculum stands at the heart of academic practice, yet it remains an underdeveloped resource of learning.

The professoriat, with other professions, earns its badge of professionalism by confronting the dilemmas of academic practice. Some of these dilemmas can be seen as products of paradoxes that are ever present but seldom acknowledged.

The first paradox is that the instrumentalities of education are almost all collective—courses, classes, programs—but the essential process of learning is highly individual. This paradox is at the root of a common frustration in educational research—no significant results (Dubin and Taveggia 1968).

A second paradox is that only the student engages the curriculum directly: Everyone else must deal with it by symbolic reference. Faculty construct the curriculum but do not live it: Students live it but have only a small part in making it (Barzun 1959, p. 88). One manifestation of this paradox is found in the tendency of academics on curriculum committees to reach back to their own undergraduate experience to apprehend the meaning of curricular alternatives.

A third paradox arises because the curriculum is oriented toward the future—it must anticipate the life ahead—but is predicated on the past. Relevance, in the fullest sense, is just beyond grasp.

The list of paradoxes might be lengthened to include collisions between research (new knowledge) and teaching (transmission of accepted knowledge), and between students' expectations and the faculty's intentions. Professionals in the academy face the same kind of dilemmas found in other professions. A field alert to professionalization will continuously face up to and analyze the dilemmas of the practice situation, in this case the curriculum. That analysis itself becomes a source of vitality.

The academic profession, large as it is and important as it has become in an information-based society, needs an effective vehicle for professionalization, some would say "reprofessionalization." "Perhaps the key to comprehending . . . American educational practice lies in the history of the professions. . . . In the end, therefore, if anything is going to be done to confront the crisis in American higher education, it is going to be done by the professors or it is not going to be done at all" (Rudolph 1984, p. 13). The professional practice situation, represented by the curriculum and its challenges, is the most promising avenue to continued professionalization. Three decades of experimentation with other dimensions of professional practice are behind us. Worthwhile achievements have been made, but none of them have substantially stimulated professionalization. Instructional development, with its focus on teaching and "instructional systems," leads back to the performance of the professor. While the technology has been enlarged, little light has been shed on the ethos of the profession or the primary functions of the institutions. Nor has the more comprehensive idea of faculty development contributed much to the revitalization of the profession as a whole—which is not to say that these orientations are not useful or necessary (see Schuster, Wheeler, et al. 1990). Few of these efforts, however, have generated the span of influence and concern needed for professionalization. The curriculum will.

A review of analyses of curricula categorizes them in terms of very specific purposes—administrative review for new courses, self-study, committee analysis, board intervention, comparative study—but contains little evidence of "theory" in action (Mayhew and Ford 1971, p. 81). This idiosyncratic approach to such analysis is still widely evident. The practice has serious shortcomings, however, in that it chops the total curriculum into pieces offering momentary convenience but results that are rarely consistent from one setting to another and seldom congruent with each other.

This monograph advocates a very different view. Analysis of the curriculum, whatever the purpose, whatever the level, is a critical feature of the practice situation in the academic profession. It follows that such analysis should follow sound organizing principles, principles consonant with academic conditions. The established professions have elaborated design into context, content, and form. The concept offers a defining principle very appropriate to the teaching-learning situation.

Changes in the curriculum to meet contemporary challenges are made in one of three ways: (1) modification or reform, the most familiar; (2) integration, perhaps the most difficult; and (3) transformation, a type of change that responds to complexity and uncertainty. A need for curricular change arises now from challenges in the external environment and from the internal complexities of management. The next section deals with how transforming actions can be worked out in two stages: a preparatory process of curriculum analysis, followed by a program of organizational change.

THE PROCESS OF ANALYSIS

Moving toward Transformation: Setting and Process
Why transformation?

Today, no shortage of challenges exists that overreach the familiar modes of curricular change, modification and integration, and demand a transformation. Experience of the past 25 years with conventional approaches to some of these challenges reinforces the importance of a transformational procedure. For example, when militant blacks in the 1960s called for the study of black issues in the curriculum, the first response was to follow the path of modification: to add a new discipline-like entity to the administrative structure, isolate the issues, and leave the advocates to fend for themselves. The approach is entirely consistent with the reductionist, positivist tradition in the academy and reflects the way new ideas have been moved into the curriculum for a hundred years (Hopmann 1991, p. 5). Women's studies in the 1970s reflect the same attempts at differentiation and segmentation within the curriculum. In both instances, however, response by modification is insufficient for the issues. Reflecting on those experiences tells us a great deal about what a transformation of the curriculum requires.

The formidable curricular issues on the doorstep of the academy now presage a very different undergraduate curriculum by 2000.

The nature of transformational issues

How can, or should, the curriculum encompass issues that promise impacts across programs and departments: gender equity, respect for racial or ethnic identity, environmental understanding and action, issues of ethics and mutual responsibility, appreciation for science and technology, comprehension of global interdependency?

These challenges share attributes that raise them to the level of curriculumwide issues and posit a need for transformation. Each has a complex structure and will not yield to simple solutions. Each requires a knowledge base that is now incomplete and largely beyond the disciplines and professional specialties that make up the curriculum. Each has significant consequences for the main functions of our society, present and future, and each carries emotional loads of great force. Finally, even though the directions that "ought" to be pursued—the moral imperatives—often are clear, the nature and shape of final outcomes are not known. At this time, even the most

---

obstinate advocate cannot know for sure what a "diversified curriculum" or a "global curriculum" looks like. We are all in a state of common inquiry.

All these features point toward a process of searching, a quest for curriculum, something more open than the well-rounded plan or statement of goals that marks strategic or long-range planning (see figure 3).

FIGURE 3

ANALYSIS OF THE CURRICULUM: Prelude to Change

Process	Content	Product
Legitimation	Of topics; of procedures	Statement of Operating Principles or Charge
Exploration	Normative information, comparative data, conceptual alternatives	Working papers, data
Synthesis	Rationale and reasonable alternatives	Proposal
Negotiation	Reactions, position papers, discussions	Reaction papers, transcripts
Arbitration/ Mediation	Evaluated alternatives for planning and action	White paper covering current conditions, rationale for change, directions

A two-stage process

The process of transformation has two distinct components. The first is exploration by *systematic analysis,* the second action for *organizational change.* It follows, therefore, that programs for changing the curriculum to meet the challenges of today are best conceived as a two-stage process. Each stage is a discrete operation.

> *Curriculum planning should be a two-tier or hierarchial process. The "postmodern" challenges [those identified with the curriculum among them] are marked by open systems thinking, a complex structure, and . . . transformatory [as opposed to accumulative] change* (Doll 1989, pp. 244, 251).

Finding examples

The most striking features of the various trials—and even the successes of curricular change—are difference and incompletion. Institutions and their faculties set a distinctive stamp on a program of study. Individualism is apparent in the AASCU's (American Association of State Colleges and Universities's) self-reports from 10 institutions that participated in APEP, the Academic Program Evaluation Project (1986). The common purpose of the project was assessing the quality of presentation, given a set of intellectual skills. In fact, as the reports show, it also afforded opportunities to reset the curriculum in a variety of ways.

Another example of large-scale change was undertaken at the University of Minnesota. The FOCUS project shows evidence of the variation generated across departments (Pazandak 1989). As a means of improving the quality of undergraduate education, four "elements of excellence" were translated into expressions that were largely curricular in nature. A testimony to the difficulties of curricular change is found in the small share of institutions that actually fulfill their intentions.

Still other kinds of change point up the variations. The search for better general education programs prompted, and still motivates, much curricular change (see, e.g., Gaff 1983). A review of practices in four-year colleges, for example, found great regularity in the amount of general education but wide variation in content and purpose (Toombs, Fairweather, et al. 1989). The papers at AAC meetings and just about every issue of *Liberal Education* report hands-on experience with attempts to revise curricula in liberal arts colleges. Few examples exist, however, of transformation in its completed form. Many institutions have initiated partial efforts in that direction, usually in a search for ways to handle diversity in the curriculum. In the area of women's studies, for example, "over 50 colleges and universities have at least the rudiments of curriculum transformation projects" (Schuster and Van Dyne 1985, p. 21). In the mid-1980s, most projects depended on external funding, emphasized faculty development (most often through workshops), and concentrated on "assuring progeny" to carry the process forward. They tended to operate in conventional modes that reflect modification rather than transformation—top-down, piggyback (infusing existing courses), or bottom-up.

Because even the proponents of transformation see the process as incomplete and also because of the immediacy of the challenges, now is a good time for open, speculative consideration about how a transforming process can be started. A particularly good theme for tracing transforming approaches

Few examples exist, however, of transformation in its completed form.

is found in the search for gender equity. The topic leaves no field or discipline untouched. Feminist challenges reach out beyond the curriculum into administrative practice and institutional policy. They postulate new modes and premises for research. The literature dealing with women in the academy provides a rich, well-articulated, and compelling body of information, exchange, and argument. Even the briefest reading of feminist literature makes clear the magnitude of the transformation that lies ahead.

> *Creating an inclusive curriculum means more than bringing women's studies into the general curriculum because it also means creating a program . . . that does not have the racist, class, heterosexist, and cultural bias that is found in the traditional curriculum* (Andersen 1988, p. 53).

That passage also raises one of the key problems for exploration and negotiation: whether it is possible to deal with all of the complexions of bias with a single transformation. Feminist scholars attach great urgency to curricular change (see, e.g., Barnard 1981; Farnham 1987; Hoffnung 1984; McIntosh 1983; Minnich, O'Barr, and Rosenfeld 1988; Schuster and Van Dyne 1985). Women, however dedicated and knowledgeable, cannot alone transform the curriculum. Collegial and institutional dimensions rise to the surface constantly. With these perspectives in mind, we turn to curriculum analysis and organizational change.

Legitimation
Principles of analysis
The process of establishing acceptance, "a condition of mutual trust," "a willingness to comply," is usually emphasized in discussions of governance and organizational behavior (Mortimer and McConnell 1978, p. 284). In that setting *legitimation* is a precondition to the distribution and exercise of authority and power. In governance, legitimacy could spring from cultural values, acceptance of the social structure, or designation by a legitimate agent (Herbert 1976, p. 91). It could rest on a basis of "expertise, formal role, personal rapport, or generalized deference to authority" (Mortimer and McConnell 1978, p. 18). Legitimation is just as crucial as the first process in curricular transformation, but here it has different functions and a very different base. The functions in this case are to establish

openness more than compliance, to achieve a *willingness to participate,* and to move *exploration* in a general direction rather than along a designated path.

Distinctions between these two definitions of legitimacy are evident in several incidents and a spate of critical reactions reported in recent months. "Professor [from Clark University] resists request to teach pluralistic views" says a headline in the *New York Times.* The faculty member reached to the heart of legitimacy: "What is before you is not meant in any way to be a referendum on pluralism. . . . Its aim is to try to re-establish some faculty control over the curriculum" (18 November 1990).

It is worth emphasizing that, in the setting of the curriculum, the "compliance" of governance is replaced by engagement, by joining up. The process is variously referred to as "buying in" or "taking ownership" or "commitment," but the core of the idea is the same. It signifies substantive as well as symbolic participation.

All who might be called on to support the potential outcomes must actively acknowledge what "problem" will be addressed. Most comprehensive curricular projects eventually present demands on constituencies beyond the faculty, touching financial offices or physical plant, for example. The individuals involved deserve to know in advance that the outcomes are viewed as serious and that they are a part of the process.

> *Fostering fundamental changes in educational programs and practices . . . requires high visibility at the top, commitment of energy and resources, a long lead time, and instructional and support staff that are convinced of the value of the changes and of their own abilities to implement them* (Pazandak 1989, p. 5).

Failure to connect with the central structures and functions dooms efforts at change—if not early, then later. The atrophy of faculty development programs has been related to insufficient links with the crucial processes like promotion and tenure and with key offices, to reduced support and recognition at the institutional level, and to an absence of rewards and compensation (Uwalaka 1986). Change in the curriculum starts with legitimation of the process among all relevant constituencies.

Hazy legitimacy is also fatal. An important corollary is that acts of legitimation need to be unambiguous. Because endorsement at the top generates the force of an "indirect stimulus" and deans often play the role of essential catalyst, the decision to participate has the quality of a "go/no go" choice. Where curricular change is part of a strategic plan, the commitment of the top level is crucial in setting directions.

Voices that lay claim to legitimacy in governance still speak in terms of "empowerment" or "control of decision making." Increasingly, however, it is apparent that this approach leads to closed positions on all sides. An adversarial posture might have some advantages in confronting the administrative structure, but, in the setting of the curriculum, it tends toward stalemate. What is really needed is participation in a process of exploration and inquiry.

Legitimation of the topic
Legitimation reaches not only the process and the participants but also the topic itself. The issue needs to carry its own rationale. To begin with, careful attention to the scope and limits under study is required. The curriculum has the qualities of a covenant—more than a promise, but less than an oath (Scott 1981). Such a covenant requires that the issue match the talent to be invested. Some issues are too specific to legitimately command the attention of an entire institution.

The AASCU project, for example, targeted "generic skills"— analysis, synthesis, quantification, communication, valuing. Important as they are, a whole institution is not likely to see them as legitimate. They belong at the level of the course, the pattern, and the constellation and could have been so defined at the outset.

A danger exists that "popular ideas" in the curriculum can become overblown. For all its value, "critical thinking lacks the creative, constructive, and design elements necessary for social progress" (DeBono 1984, p. 16). Shallow "curriculum development," goals leading to mediocrity, and comprehensive topics that concentrate on the full scope of "education" should be carefully distinguished (Klein 1983).

In contrast, some issues are too large to be covered entirely by a project on curricular change. The extensive and profound considerations raised by feminist studies are perhaps the best example of an issue completely entwined with the curriculum, on the one hand, and demanding of analysis and action in many other sectors of the academy and the institution, on the other. The extra-academic community, with its demographic, legal, and cultural changes for women, actively interacts with the academic community. A direct challenge to the scope of knowledge affects scholarship and disciplines across the board: "We are coming to see that academic learning is incomplete, biased, and parochial" (Barnard 1981).

> *Since women have been excluded from the creation of formalized knowledge, to include women means more than just adding women into existing knowledge or making them new objects of knowledge. . . . Including women refers to the complex process of redefining knowledge by making women's experiences a primary subject for knowledge, conceptualizing women as active agents in the creation of knowledge, including women's perspectives on knowledge, looking at gender as fundamental to the articulation of knowledge in Western thought, and seeing women's and men's experiences in relation to the sex/gender system. Feminists in educational institutions will likely continue working for both women's studies and curriculum change, since both projects seek to change the content and form of the traditional curriculum* (Andersen 1988, pp. 38, 53).

Curricular transformation, it must be recognized, often stands as one essential and discrete part of a much larger transformation. Exactly the same circumstances are inherent in racial and ethnic considerations. Curricular change is only one legitimate topic on the agenda, and it does not override or substitute for other legitimate concerns, such as African-American or Hispanic studies. Choosing the right scope, a level of concentration that carries logical coherence, and precisely the right issues confers the legitimacy of subjects on curricular transformation.

Operational considerations
Practical considerations arise at this point: Who will do the work? By what means is legitimation established? What will the first products be? Analysis of the curriculum is one area of academic life where the nature of decision making is indisputably collegial. Initiatives on restructuring arise most frequently with the faculty, roughly 40 to 50 percent of the cases, but that still leaves plenty of room for guidance and reactions

from other contributors (Franklin 1988, p. 204). The theme of shared and differentiated decision making places a high premium on "reasoning together," a hallmark of the collegial model (Chaffee 1983, p. 15). Within the loose collegial model are choices to be made about the mode of operation. Somehow higher education has become fixated on the blue-ribbon-committee-with-recommendations as a preferred device.

Legitimation calls for wide participation as well as specific actions. The plan of operation at the legitimizing stage requires plenary representation. Inventiveness is also important. One popular mode of operation begins with the establishment of a steering committee whose responsibilities include oversight, internal communication, and evaluation. Other options include a staff office with continuing representation and support personnel whose principal task is to move the project forward. An ad hoc convening body can also serve as the agent for establishing legitimacy.

Whatever the mechanism for oversight, the first tangible product in the process of curricular analysis is a legitimating document, a "charge," "articles of agreement," or "operating assumptions." The purpose is to establish a consensual foundation, a direction, for the entire project.

Exploration
Operations
Engagement and imagination are so valuable at the working level that models other than the executive model of chairman and subordinate members deserve consideration. Once the main topics are laid out, the format for the task units can be chosen. Consensual models, nonauthoritarian models that use group process techniques to generate information along with staff support for collation and feedback, proved effective with autonomous professionals in a variety of fields (Smutz 1984). Highly focused task groups or subcommittees within a task force accompanied by networking and frequent intercommunication give the flexibility to deal with specific topics. A major effort to change the curriculum at Monmouth College (Education for Leadership and Social Responsibility) is developing a variety of techniques for linking faculty, administration, and community (Nemerowicz and Rosi 1990).

When patterns of proprietary interest are strong, it might be necessary to use "stake-holder" groups as the working units. A functional distribution of activities in the exploratory stage—description, information gathering, synthesis—might be useful. The social dynamics of size deserve strict attention: five to seven members for action and decision, eight to twelve members for deliberation, 12 to 20 members for communication sessions. Larger numbers operate as an audience.

Developing possibilities and alternatives

The operation of any curriculum has an inherent tendency for isolation and segmentation to accumulate across the courses. As a consequence, most activities that involve the curriculum—accreditation, strategic planning, program review—start with *description,* a forthright statement of what is going on. Fortunately, much of the information is often at hand. By casting or recasting the material into the framework of design (context, content, and form) then abstracting common features, useful statements can be generated.

No one wants to reinvent the wheel when engaged in a time-consuming and complex activity. The only reasonable way to avoid it is to marshal the best and most timely information and put it to as many uses as possible. Inevitably, many faculty can contribute expertise from their own field about how the profession has dealt with the topic and what efforts other institutions have made. In the case of gender equity, for example, the importance of infusing teaching, learning, and research with a feminist component has been widely reported. Full-time staff support is imperative in this information-gathering stage, and special costs exist in the acquisition, synthesis, and distribution of new information.

Lost, misused, or wasted time is the enemy of every deliberative body. Much of the material generated for curricular change can serve in accreditation or program review. A careful recording of events is vital for communication, external as well as internal. Written status reports, widely circulated, are familiar. Academics have not drawn much on the well of communication technology for day-to-day business, except in research. Entering reports into an open data file on a computer network provides for interactive response and a running commentary. Since audio tapes made the Iranian revolution possible and the fax machine sustained the events in Tiananmen Square, the communicative power of new technologies can hardly be doubted.

Not all information is equal. Of special importance is information that encourages wide perspectives on the curriculum

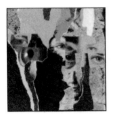

beyond the limited viewpoints of discipline and course. Two kinds of information with such value are *normative data* and *comparative data.* Fortunately, the published sources of information in both categories have multiplied in the last decade. Normative data give a sense of variation and central tendency. Questions dealing with courses listed per faculty member, departmental size, amount of credits for majors, minors, and "service" courses often come up when change is discussed. Comparative data display conditions at one institution in contrast to practices at similar institutions. Purely analytical treatment of data to describe the current situation in terms of critical ratios, courses listed versus courses offered, listings per faculty by department, and so on is valuable.

Normative information on curricular practice describes the range and concentration of use for a particular feature. The data gathered by the Carnegie Foundation and periodically amended provides facts about credit distributions, courses listed per faculty member, and department size (Levine 1981), providing an excellent background against which to examine one's own program. The American Council on Education's fact books are a mine of information on the shifting patterns of students' choices by major. The recent faculty surveys by the Office of Educational Research and Improvement provide a wealth of comparative information on faculty work styles. The successive surveys of the Carnegie Foundation provide timely summaries of practice. From the National Center for Education Statistics, the series on the condition of education, published since 1975, provide more summary data on general practices. The data files available through the *Chronicle of Higher Education* and the frequent summaries published in *Chance* merit examination. And several efforts at transcript analysis, notably at the University of Pennsylvania and at Penn State University, will soon provide considerable information on the actual patterns of students' choices.

A similar wealth of qualitative source materials is available (see, e.g., Cohen et al. 1986 for a review of material on junior and community colleges; Menges and Mathis 1988 for information on teaching and learning; Schubert 1980 for a list of books on the curriculum beginning in about 1960; Schuster, Wheeler, et al. 1990 for a chapter providing a thorough compilation of works on faculty development; and Stark and Lowther 1986 for an indispensable review of the literature). Of special value is the "custom computer search" provided by the ERIC Clearinghouse. Timely and comprehensive, these products are particularly useful in identifying parallel endeavors. Matthew Arnold once observed that an afternoon in the library could make one the second best-informed person in the world on any given subject. That option now exists with respect to normative data and source materials on curricular practices. A studied information base of normative data and sources can go far toward establishing a common background of understanding.

Synthesis

It is at the point of synthesis that the transformative approach makes a distinctive contribution. A major working paper summarizing the explorations in the form of alternatives provides the substance for negotiation and exchange until the priorities among the alternatives are worked out. A foundation for programs of action, for organizational change, is generated. The product is a *position paper* with the scope and independence of a "white paper." Reflecting the processes that produced it, the document opens with a *description* of current practice, followed by a section reporting essential *information* from the research. The final section brings together an array of *alternatives* that point in the desired directions. They are not yet plans for action but alternative scenarios that can form the basis for exchange and negotiation. Each task group and all interest groups contribute, but the final paper is best generated by a staff group or a "writing team" whose task is synthesis, not invention.

Goals, plans for action, stipulations of mission and purpose are not yet specific. This procedure might seem drawn out, but, given the complexity of curricular transformation and the collaborative nature of the process, broad coverage has more value than specificity. It is agreement on *directions* rather than goals for action that is the first outcome.

Negotiation

Negotiation is always part of organizational change, of curricular change in particular. Often it goes unacknowledged or undervalued by academics who prefer to negotiate from a position of criticism after plans of action are drawn up. At that stage, confronted by fixed fiats for change, the instruments of negotiation are often limited to resistance and vetoes, foot dragging, and quiet subversion. Undergoing nego-

---

tiation before an action plan is set and focusing on alternatives and priorities ensure a sounder basis for the acts of change. Neglect of this piece of the process has its price.

Again, the challenge of introducing gender equity into the curriculum offers an example. The tendency is for curricular change to get bogged down in intermediate stages (McIntosh 1983). Organizations tend to have a native rate of absorption for new practices, and negotiation helps keep it moving.

With respect to the processes of exploration—the development of new information, theory, examples, and analysis—the efforts of women's studies are strikingly successful. Issues are presented in a rich literature that is readily accessible. The directions, as in the notion of an "inclusive curriculum," are well explored (Andersen 1988). The practical problem is how to bring considerations of gender to a negotiating table—to the department, courses, patterns, and constellations. The present stage of transformation toward gender equity in the curriculum has plenty of room for negotiation. The alternatives developed by exploration will inevitably cover a wide range of directions.

One line of alternatives in this case is likely to reflect an ultrarevisionist view that " . . . to see through the androcentric veil, we must shift to another paradigm" (Farnham 1987, p. 53). The call for a new vision is sweeping, challenging notions of "canon," "values," "authority," and "form," setting aside claims of "objective," "rational," "analytical," and "dispassionate" scholarship as a mask for an invisible paradigm. At the modest end of the proposals is the idea that the content of courses can be infused with examples of women's contributions to the field.

Any change in thinking of the magnitude involved in such topics will be evolutionary, and the initial negotiation is only a beginning. The disciplinary department or comparable unit of a professional program is the best place for negotiation (Farnham 1987; Schuster and Van Dyne 1985). "A distinguishing characteristic . . . is the locus for change. They operate within the departmental or divisional structure, which is particularly useful as a base for imagining alternatives to those structures [that] not only tend to isolate individuals but to fragment knowledge" (Schuster and Van Dyne 1985, p. 34). The product of negotiation is an assignment of priorities among the alternatives, a prelude to organizational change.

Retrospection

The term "retrospection" was selected to emphasize that evaluation of curricular change involves observation as well as measured assessment or summative evaluation. Monitoring, tracking, and recording events are part of retrospection. Continuous reflection is emphasized (see Argyris and Schon 1978). The AASCU's report offers a notable piece of retrospection in several respects. First, it demonstrates that the processes of curricular change, however similar the starting point, can generate a widely variable set of outcomes, and serendipity plays a large role. Second, as a nonjudgmental description, it allows us to see for ourselves, to learn, from a series of related events. Third, retrospection helps unearth the "hidden curriculum," the filtering and interpretive forces of unwitting action and the patterns of counterinfluence that sometime underlie efforts.

A place for structured assessment of the curriculum as well as its outcomes of course exists. Apart from the analysis of student outcomes in terms of performance is a series of assessment questions to be applied at critical junctures of developing the curriculum. How well does the form of the program fit with content? Are the full implications of context considered? How well do the mechanics of structure—class, course, text, lab—reflect the intentions of the designers? Do the actual operation, course schedules, and sequences conform to the design's intentions?

In summary, undertaking a transformation of the curriculum requires more preparatory effort than other kinds of planned change. Accurate description, careful legitimation of topic and process, exploration of new views and information, and negotiation must be carefully thought out before acting. The instrumentality best suited to the process is a kind of white paper offering alternative directions that can be negotiated into a set of guiding priorities, yielding a framework for organizational change.

MANAGING CHANGE IN THE CURRICULUM

"We do not understand enough about how changes are effected in individual practice or in the nature of institutions to give definite, well-tested guidelines" (Mayhew and Ford 1971, p. 110). Although organizational change has become a key topic in the literature on organizational theory and the implementation of curricular reform has become a central concern to curricular theorists, this statement is still true. In large part because many different constituencies have deeply held beliefs about institutional curricula, the administrator or faculty member who wishes to alter the curriculum still lacks a general schema about how to manage change. We do know a series of questions that should be asked, information that should be gathered, and models of curricular decision making that can be called upon, however, when an organization's participants intend to undertake a review of the curriculum.

This section first reviews theories of change from an organizational viewpoint and then discusses ideas about curricular change. Both reviews highlight how different theoretical perspectives orient the change processes one can use and the obstacles encountered to implementing academic change. The section concludes with the roles different constituencies might play in curricular change and questions and schemes that might be developed to orchestrate change successfully.

Planning Organizational Change
Defining change
Change can be defined as the processes of applying a new idea to create a new process or product. By inducing change in the organization, the organizational participants are working in an environment that in many ways is opposite from an organizational environment built on stable processes and outcomes. "The task of the innovating organization is fundamentally different from that of the operating organization" (Galbraith 1982, p. 5). That is, an innovating organization constantly reconfigures its outcomes and goals, which in turn could necessitate different organizational processes to achieve those outcomes and goals. Consequently, the innovating organization possesses different characteristics from a stable organization; in an innovating organization, a high degree of uncertainty and risk is involved, and failure is more likely than in an operating organization. At the same time, commitment

might be higher and the rewards greater in an organization that stresses innovation and change.

Three major theoretical perspectives of the organization concern change and innovation—technological, political, and cultural (Firestone and Corbett 1988)—(although a different perspective could be useful under different conditions). Before undertaking curricular change, one needs to diagnose the organization to understand the processes guiding it.

The *technological* perspective views implementation as a rational, technical process. The assumption is that organizations have a single set of clear goals that will be adapted to the demands of the external environment. The *political* perspective emphasizes the incentives and balances of power among organizational participants with divergent interests. The *cultural* perspective is a relatively new viewpoint stressing the enduring values and traditions of individuals involved in change. An organization's culture establishes a set of long-standing and often implicit criteria for assessment that an innovation must meet to be accepted.

This monograph works from the assumption that an organization's culture is a critical element as it directs and regulates individuals' behavior. That is, existing norms and values are inherent in the institution's culture. Beliefs are often difficult to change because they give intrinsic meaning to organizational activity (Firestone, Corbett, and Rossman 1987). The assumption underlying this perspective is that organizational cultures are conservative and thus present obstacles to efforts at curricular reform that conflict with cultural norms.

Researchers recently have suggested that an awareness of each perspective is a necessary strategy to induce organizational change (Chaffee 1989; Chaffee and Tierney 1988). The successful change agent understands what adaptations the organization must undergo to meet the needs of external constituencies; the organization's internal political processes are understood so that, to the extent possible, rational decision making occurs. Finally, and most important, the change agent successfully interprets the culture of the organization to internal constituencies so that the constituents participate in and understand the changes that need to take place. The overriding assumption is that in a turbulent environment an understanding of that environment and the continuous interpretation of the organization's relationship to it are critical to achieving organizational effectiveness.

A framework of change

To successfully orchestrate change in the organization, one must draw on a series of tactics that incorporate technological, political, and cultural perspectives. These tactics can be systematized into a framework that contains four major components: (1) structure and roles, (2) organizational processes, (3) incentives, and (4) idea champions (Galbraith 1982). The first component, structure and roles, includes three major roles—leaders, sponsors, and orchestrators—who focus on the technological and political perspectives. Individuals adopt these roles and interact with one another to bring about change. An understanding of the organization's structures and roles essentially enables one to comprehend how ideas should be introduced, argued about, and decided upon if change is to take place. Who is responsible for monitoring the environment and comprehending the needs of external constituencies is investigated. The role of the organization's leader and a structural understanding of who holds the political power to sponsor ideas and foment change are key considerations.

The second organizational component, organizational processes, focuses on the key processes of funding, acquiring new ideas, combining ideas, moving ideas to the operating organization, and managing change. Once one understands the structure of decision making, how the structure is enacted gains importance. This component highlights cultural and political perspectives. What are the normative processes required for action to occur? What symbolic activities must take place for an idea to be implemented?

The third component, incentives, encourages innovating behavior. Innovating organizations need to develop a reward system that attracts and retains idea people to the organization, provides the motivation for attempts to innovate, and rewards successful performance. The clearest difference between an innovating and an operating organization is in how different organizations reward incentives. Innovating organizations develop strategies to reward new ideas, while operating organizations reward other activities; in some instances, disincentives exist in an operating organization that wishes to maintain stability and avoid innovation.

The fourth component, idea champions, focuses on how the organization identifies and develops individuals who generate ideas (Daft and Becker 1978). Idea champions are those

What symbolic activities must take place for an idea to be implemented?

individuals who not only develop an idea, but also have the desire and determination to see the idea through. Idea champions do not have to reside in the upper echelons of the hierarchy; as an innovation moves through the structural component, however, support from organizational leaders and sponsors is necessary. The assumption that idea champions reside throughout the organization rather than only in senior roles has far-ranging implications. Incentives, for example, will be developed for all individuals in the organization so that everyone will perceive that part of his or her role is to develop new ideas and strategies.

In sum, a central theme of much of the literature on organizational change is that innovating organizations must be specifically designed to innovate. The innovation design needs to incorporate technological, political, and cultural aspects. Thus, organizations must plan for innovation by the formal development of these critical components. By understanding the organizational perspectives and the general framework for innovation, one can better understand why resistance occurs to planned changes and what strategies to use to overcome obstacles to curricular change.

Planning Curricular Change

A wealth of literature has been developed about managing academic change (see, e.g., Chickering et al. 1977; Conrad 1978; Dill and Friedman 1979; Hefferlin 1969; Levine 1980; Lindquist 1978). This subsection is limited to a discussion of the four stages an innovation goes through before its acceptance and seven barriers to change.

Stages of curricular change

Understanding that an innovation moves through various stages means that an organization's participants can decide which different organizational levers should be called upon to move the process along (see Levine 1980 and 1981 for perhaps the most helpful works in understanding different curricular innovations and the stages an innovation goes through before its formal acceptance). Different stages demand different degrees of participation, and if we understand the point where an innovative idea is, then we will be better able to come to terms with who should be involved.

The stages begin with the recognition of a need. We expect that the environment will determine many of an organization's needs. At the same time, the culture of the organization will help frame how the need is initially presented and framed. The second stage is the plan and formulation of a solution. Both of these stages involve participation that can vary from the entire organization to certain individuals.

The third stage is the trial period when the innovation is implemented. The last stage is either institutionalization, when the innovation becomes a routine part of the organization, or termination. The third and fourth stages often receive the least consideration by organizational participants. How to determine whether an experiment is successful or who will decide whether the innovation should be formally accepted are questions that demand consideration.

Like the cultural model, a basic assumption inherent in Levine's model is the recognition that each organization has a distinctive set of norms, values, and goals that constitutes its personality or character. The success or failure of an innovation might in large part be the result of the organization's norms. It is helpful to consider the stages of innovation in terms of the framework for change mentioned earlier. Several questions combine the stages and the frameworks:

- What are the incentives that create a climate for innovation in the first stage?
- Is the idea champion someone who has the stamina and wherewithal to foster the innovation through all four stages?
- At what point should the leader become involved?
- What is the structure that will allow for effective and efficient decisions in the second stage?
- How have the processes for assessment been designed for the third stage?
- Who will decide whether the experiment will be incorporated into the organization?

Barriers to change
Seven major findings bear directly on the organizational barriers to implementing curricular change (see, e.g., Hefferlin 1969; Levine 1980; Lindquist 1978; Martorana and Kuhns 1975). Once we understand the barriers to change, we can come to terms with how to overcome those obstacles.

First, resistance to innovation is related to organizational stability (Levine 1980). By its very nature, an innovation will attempt to change the boundaries of the organization. Unstable organizations or institutions in crisis are more likely to be willing to have permeable boundaries. "In stable or rigid organizations, [however,] innovations are more likely to be perceived as incompatible, unprofitable, or both" (Levine 1980, p. 169). The conflict brought about by the change will ultimately be resolved by either the inclusion or termination of the change. Thus, instability tends to be a critical element to consider for the innovative organization.

Second, resistance to innovation is associated primarily with two organizational variables: those pertaining to issues of formalization (centralization) and profitability (stratification of rewards, emphasis on efficiency, and job satisfaction). In short, the more centralization, rules, bureaucratic procedures, and formalization that occur, the less likely are innovations to occur. The more stratification or wide disparity in the distribution of rewards from the top to bottom of the organization, the less likely it will be for innovation to take place. A stratified organization will not provide incentives for all stake holders to think of themselves as idea champions.

Third, resistance to innovation is related to the organization's culture. Cultures are inherently conservative and not prone to accept dramatic ideas or actions. An organization's culture is determined by its history and the various organizational elements that comprise it (Tierney 1988a) and interpret it. The assumption is that how the participants interpret their environment, for example, or what innovations are needed are in large part determined by the organization's culture. The point is not that strong cultures resist change and weak cultures do not; rather, organizational leaders must come to terms with understanding the culture if they want to create a climate for change. How members are socialized, the reward structure, the traditions and overarching mission, the manner in which the leader creates and conveys organizational meaning, and a host of other cultural variables all go a long way toward determining how the institution's participants perceive new ideas.

A fourth barrier concerns inertia and fear of the unknown. In this light, the maintenance of what is current is difficult enough without trying to implement anything else that inevitably involves organizational and individual risks. "College leaders, like truckers on steep grades, have all they can do to keep their institution on the road" (Lindquist 1978, p. 114).

teaching. Unless someone takes responsibility for marshaling a curricular change through the various stages, the status quo will prevail.

A fifth barrier concerns the lack of relevant information decision makers hold about a problem. Information about what should or should not be included in a college curriculum is often anecdotal (Mayhew and Ford 1971). Projections about students' attendance, aptitudes, and needs—especially in a turbulent environment—often lack statistical accuracy, so that decisions about the curriculum often turn on philosophical conjecture rather than empirical evidence.

A sixth disincentive to change in academe is that a postsecondary institution's reputation is in general not based on innovation. Unlike a profit-making company that needs to offer different automobiles or a different line of fashion to meet consumers' changing needs, a postsecondary organization often bases its reputation on its history (Hefferlin 1969). An institution that adopts broad curricular changes is in danger of tampering with how different audiences conceive of the organization.

The seventh barrier relates to a traditional problem of academe: Lines of decision-making authority are unclear. Curricular decision-making bodies are often unwieldy in size, and the time needed to suggest a new idea, debate its pros and cons, work the idea through the various deliberative bodies of the institution, and finally implement the change could take years. The stages of an innovation might move along so slowly that the participants will view success when a decision has been reached; the ramifications of how the innovation will be implemented and assessed might not be thought through—and might be the responsibility of no one. The perception could arise that all the organizational participants have done is talk about change rather than implement it if, at the end of an academic year, no action has been taken other than affirm the status quo.

Implementing Curricular Change
Previous discussions
The problem with any "recipe for successful change" (Levine 1980, p. 190) is that each cook has his or her own way of interpreting the ingredients and each cook's oven varies in temperature. One's tools and interpretation could drastically

alter the nature of any recipe. Nevertheless, those who want to implement successful change have been encouraged to take several factors into account:

- Create a climate, even a demand, for change.
- Diminish the threat associated with innovation and avoid hard-line approaches.
- Avoid being timid.
- Appreciate timing.
- Gear the innovation to the organization.
- Disseminate and evaluate information.
- Communicate effectively.
- Get organizational leaders behind the innovation.
- Build a base of active support.
- Establish rewards.
- Plan for the period after adoption.

The problem with a laundry list of this sort is that the change agent has no systematic way of incorporating what he or she must do to bring about curricular change (Levine 1980). This section now suggests a schema for implementing change that synthesizes the organization's perspectives, the framework for change, the stages of change, and the barriers to it. The schema is based on four assumptions. First, innovative organizations must be designed; they are fundamentally different from operating organizations built on stability and repetition. Second, ongoing analysis rather than evaluation is key, for an innovative organization is always undergoing change and analysis, compared to operating organizations, which might operate successfully with periodic evaluations. Third, curricular change should come about not because of a state of dissatisfaction (Wood and Davis 1978), but because the state of curricular operations is in continuous review. Fourth, the manner in which the organization is organized is critical for successful innovation.

Two caveats come with this list. First, postsecondary organizations most often are not designed to be innovative. The culture, history, inertia, and decision-making structures of colleges and universities often mitigate against overhauling the curriculum. Organizational participants often see curricular discussions as a gratuitous waste of time that should be undertaken only at the behest of external demands, such as the need to write an accreditation report.

Second, a cultural perspective of the organization assumes that all organizations are distinctive; causal relationships do not exist. Causally determined guidelines cannot be developed for the innovation-minded manager, for a how-to recipe implies that innovation is complete at a particular time. Developing an innovative organization is a long-range undertaking that must be ongoing to be effective. A diagnostic frame of reference has three components: incentives, idea champions, and structure.

Steps toward an innovative organization
Building incentives. Organizational participants need to recognize that their efforts toward curricular innovation will be rewarded and valued. If we accept that a barrier to change is organizational stability and inertia, then we must necessarily think about how to encourage creative thought and action. As opposed to an organization that searches for unitary syntheses, the organization's participants must be encouraged to develop alternative interpretations.

Rewards can come about in any number of ways, but three are offered here. First, financial incentives like summer supplements are one way to communicate to faculty that the time they spend developing new ideas is appreciated. Second, providing faculty and other interested constituencies with the resources to investigate curricular efforts on other campuses or to discuss a particular topic on their own campus helps create a climate for change. Third, the ability of leaders to communicate orally and in writing their appreciation of efforts toward curricular change is an essential component for creating a climate for change.

Most individuals are aware of their institutions' fiscal constraints. In general, the expectation on campuses is not that huge sums of money must be invested for individuals to buy into efforts to change, but that success comes from a culture where an incentive for change is a central thrust.

Relatively small inducements, such as summer salaries or a partial reduction in course load to partake in a faculty seminar, are potent symbols that the organization values change. Similarly, what an administration applauds or ignores enables the participants to interpret the organization's direction and goals. The need to create an ongoing dialogue within the organization, rather than merely a response to a particular suggestion or demand, is paramount.

Speaking about the need to build incentives within the organization indirectly suggests some initiatives that might be downplayed. If resources are to be spent, the administration would be better advised to spend the resources on the participants within the organization like the faculty so that they are able to develop their own ideas about what needs to be done, rather than pay consultants to offer opinions about what needs to be done with the curriculum. The assumption is twofold. First, individuals who make decisions in part draw on their own experiences when they decide whether to implement different curricular initiatives. Providing faculty and administrators with the opportunity to visit other campuses or to discuss specific issues across disciplines aids individuals to see other views that they might not have had otherwise.

Second, enabling participants to develop their own decisions creates an atmosphere at the outset that the decision is a group activity owned by everyone. Creating a climate for curricular change necessitates that the organization's participants buy into the process. Solutions suggested by outsiders are often resisted or ignored (Tierney 1989b). National reports, accreditation requirements, state mandates, and the like could necessitate momentary changes in the curriculum, but a climate for change will not have been created. The point is not for the organization's participants to avoid the external environment in their curricular initiatives; indeed, it is essential for participants to understand the various currents at work in the larger environment. The manner in which they come to understand those currents, however, should be by the participants' ability to investigate the various changes and suggestions rather than by consultants' or authors' offering opinions about what should be done.

Idea champions. Much has been written about the need for leaders to reestablish authority within the organization (Kerr and Gade 1987). The role of a leader in an innovative organization is to promote the idea that all individuals can become leaders. To foment ideas, the organization must foster an atmosphere where everyone's ideas are valued.

This suggestion runs contrary to the cultures of some institutions, where, for example, seniority and/or presidential authority is given precedence over all other values in the organization. The point is not to disregard one's senior colleagues or to silence a president. Those who have a long history with the organization must be heard, for they will have valuable perspectives about the past, and any college president has a special perspective on the institution that should be articulated to the community. To ignore new ideas from junior faculty or younger administrators, however, is to reenforce the discussion about compatibility and profitability as barriers to change. In essence, a climate for innovation will encourage all individuals to be colearners in the organization.

Suggesting that all individuals might conceive of part of their role as developing new ideas also asserts that faculty should become more active in decision making. To be sure, examples of top-down models that started with administrative directives for sweeping curricular change have been successful, but at times the reassertion of administrative authority will be met with skepticism, if not failure.

The role of a leader in an innovative organization is to promote the idea that all individuals can become leaders.

The top-down model almost inevitably generates faculty resistance and even backlash if the administrative initiative is perceived as an effort to tell faculty members what and how to teach. The best strategy for countering that resistance . . . is to minimize the top-down nature of the project by making participation voluntary and soliciting a wide range of faculty-designed proposals to compete for available resources (Schuster and Van Dyne 1985, p. 84).

The assumption that all organizational participants have ideas that could prove to be successful innovations is in line with previous research (Daft and Becker 1978). One's status in the organization has little relation to whether a suggestion will ultimately be implemented. For the concept of an idea champion to be successful, two requirements must be met. First, idea champions not only must believe in the innovation but also must be willing to persist and invest time and energy into nurturing the idea through the various stages. Second, the idea champion needs sponsorship from influential individuals. The first requirement is met in an organization that encourages creativity by incentives. The second requirement necessitates a discussion of the structure of the decision-making process and the roles of different organizational leaders.

Structure and roles. The last decade produced a great volume of literature on academic management (see, e.g., Bennett

1983; Ehrle and Bennett 1988; Tucker 1984; Tucker and Bryan 1988). These books subscribe to the notion that academic administrators are managers, individuals who try to manage both people and resources effectively. Although the evidence for strong academic leadership is rare (Birnbaum 1988; Cohen and March 1974; Tierney 1988b), most authors still exhibit a proclivity for wanting presidents and deans to assert a clear direction for the institution (Bok 1986). Rather than yet another call for assertive academic leadership, what is called for are administrators who think more of the symbolic aspects of the organization they might call to reform and less of themselves as strong-willed leaders. Leaders might think of themselves more as orchestra conductors than as generals, more as intellectuals engaged in a creative task than as managers engaged in effective administrative practices.

"A successful strategy of reform must enlist professors in individual institutions to work together to improve . . . the curriculum. Such efforts are distressingly rare" (Bok 1986, p. 59). Especially with curricular change, administrative leaders need to promote strategies that engage the collectivity in discussions about what they want the institution to become as well as what the institution is at present. Advocating that leaders foment discussion and use symbolic processes is not to suggest that academic administrators silence their own perspectives on what curricular initiatives should be implemented. The point, however, is that rather than operating from a top-down model of decision making, administrators need to see themselves more as facilitators in a process.

Activities that can create collective dialogue range from written articles disseminated to the faculty, formal all-college meetings about a specific curricular issue, and informal faculty get-togethers or colloquia where faculty could be informed of and then discuss new ideas. Faculty life in general revolves around the individual's discipline; most faculty are not aware of many of the newest initiatives or reforms that have been advocated. The ability of the administration to provide national data and information that compare one's specific institution to the norm is critical.

At the outset of a curricular initiative, administrative action should begin with the delineation of what is expected, the time frame in which the discussion should take place, the decision-making processes and structure in which the discussion should take place, and what will occur once the decision has been reached. Thus, the discussion about the curriculum will be undertaken with the expectation that *a goal will be reached.*

The administration necessarily needs to communicate that it supports the discussion (Wood and Davis 1978, p. 44). Further, given the confused lines of decision-making authority in postsecondary institutions, at the outset of a curricular initiative all members should clearly understand the process and structure of the discussion. The different stages an initiative passes through also necessitate that the faculty should be aware of not only the time frame within which they should orient their work, but also what will be expected of the experiment once it has been agreed that it should be implemented. How will the curricular experiment be assessed? Who will be responsible for deciding whether the experiment is a success or failure?

As the discussion begins, a variety of questions should be continuously asked about the different ideas (cf. Wood and Davis 1978, pp. 40–41):

1. What is the institution's mission, and how does the curriculum fulfill that role?
2. Who is the curriculum for? Does the curriculum serve the institution's past constituency, present constituency, and/ or future constituency?
3. What information needs to be developed that will provide insight into the problems that have been defined?
4. How will the curriculum be taught? Does the current faculty have the skills necessary to implement the change? If not, what must be done?
5. How broad is the support for the initiative?
6. How will the curriculum be implemented and assessed?

Each of these questions entails more than simple checklists that individuals mark as discussion occurs. Instead, the questions should frame curricular discussions, and the discussants should continually return to them.

The question concerning the mission of the institution is of concern from both the technological and the cultural perspectives. Participants need to understand what they are about so they develop curricular initiatives that meet the technological mandates of their institution as well as the culturally specific logic with which they guide their lives. A religious institution, for example, should understand how its mission is enacted by way of the curriculum. Similarly, a state college whose mission is to serve the needs of the working class in its area must continually assess what the region's job opportunities are so that its youth can obtain gainful employment upon graduation.

A curriculum that does not serve institutional purposes ultimately creates cultural and technological imbalances that will harm different areas within the institution. The implication should not be that institutional missions do not change; indeed, suggesting that the organization's participants discuss the mission when they speak of curricular change is a call for an increased understanding of how institutional ideology is a dynamic construct.

Related to the concerns about mission is a question about the institution's constituency. A curriculum that has not changed in 20 years, or even a decade, currently might be serving a completely different clientele from the one it was designed for. Similarly, a curricular initiative based on present concerns could be outdated in five years if the environment is projected to change dramatically. The kinds of information about students that a curriculum committee needs relate to this question. Baseline data about incoming students, such as SAT scores, high school GPAs, where students come from, and the like, must be developed and compared as curricular discussions take place. What happens to students once they enter the institution—what they major in, how many credit hours they take, whether they transfer, drop out, or graduate— also must be generated.

Information should be collected and disseminated gradually as individuals come to realize what specific information they want and why they want it. Too often, information overwhelms a committee and confuses its task; information also can be used to obfuscate a problem and convince individuals of a particular argument. Information should be tied to a committee's specific questions so that individuals comprehend the information they have rather than gathering it simply for information's sake. The point is not to withhold information that will help a group reach a decision but to provide individuals with specific data that will facilitate decision making.

The concern about implementing a new curriculum relates most clearly to the political and cultural aspects of the organization. Any curricular decision that threatens the security of the present faculty will be met with resistance. Similarly, participants need to be aware at the outset of their discussions about the ramifications of their decisions. Clearly, few institutions could afford an innovation that would cost a million dollars to implement. The fact that constraints have been placed on a curricular discussion should not dissuade discussants from attempting far-ranging proposals. Rather, the discussion needs to be framed within defined parameters so that creative ideas can be grafted onto initial proposals. Faculty development or a gradual phasing in of a proposal over a number of years could ensure that initiatives eventually succeed.

Two dangers arise with innovation. On the one hand, an initiative supported by a small minority has few chances of success. On the other hand, an attempt to achieve institutional consensus appears far-fetched and ill-advised. Faculty have diverse opinions, and the expectation that all will agree on the nature of undergraduate education should be avoided in all institutions except those with the most specific institutional ideology.

Still, broad-based support is a necessity. Obviously, any idea that will take root will need active and vocal support from a variety of institutional actors. At the same time, an atmosphere should be created so that constituencies are not polarized. The expectations should be that people can disagree with the outcome of a decision and that they will be able to have a voice in the assessment of the experiment but that they will also be expected to support the initial decision.

Assessment should be an ongoing concern for both the institution's curriculum in general and specific curricular initiatives (see Banta 1988; Ewell 1984, 1985; Pace 1979 for discussions of institutional outcomes). At the beginning of their discussions, participants should have a reasonable expectation that any innovation that ultimately is implemented will have a fair and impartial assessment. Broad support for how the assessment will occur will also aid in participants' buying into the overall project.

SUMMARY

Projects dealing with the curriculum are distinctly different from other areas of institutional concern. Planning for the allocation of resources, faculty development programs, institutional advancement, and enrollment strategies, for example, all begins with a consideration of general goals and specific objectives. It rests on assumptions that the participants are wholly familiar with the process and premises.

Curricular transformation confronts another agenda. In the face of general directions pointed out compellingly by society at large and changes in the nature of knowledge, curricular objectives that fit the future needs of current students are rarely self-evident or specific. Agreement is widespread that large changes are in the offing, but even among the most experienced academics a vision of the outcomes is still amorphous. Given that topics like racial justice, ethnic diversity, and respect for the ecosphere are acceptable as broad social goals and that they belong in educational programs, how can they be read and translated into the curriculum and its components?

Many of the questions overreach the disciplinary structure of knowledge that has been the mainstay of curricular design. Many require articulated action across the curriculum, pointing to a planning approach that is process-oriented and exploratory. To borrow a phrase from the market place, "front-end loading" dominates any plan for transforming the curriculum. Thus, planning for transformation really involves two stages, one that makes an explicit analysis to clarify processes that often can be assumed in other kinds of planning, finding legitimacy, opening discourse, and negotiating principles of action that might or might not stand the long-term test. Second is the act of implementation itself, an action that deals directly with the intricacies of organizational change.

Because the first stage of a curricular transformation engages topics that are often taken for granted, the fundamentals of definition and labeling are important. Those involved in curricular change must do the same on their own campuses. The product of this first stage is a white paper that lays out the crucial dimensions of a problem in the curriculum by describing current conditions, expands on the main ideas and rationales, provides new information, and presents alternative scenarios. It forms the basis for negotiation and leads to a set of priorities.

Certain aspects take on fundamental importance. The charge—the delineation of duties and direction of inquiry—is, familiarly, put forward by the convening authority. At the outset, what is to be accomplished, who is to be involved, and how it is to be evaluated must be given full consideration. A working definition of the curriculum and its parts lays out the scope of institutional responsibility and general intentions, and acknowledges the "satisficing" nature of the curricular artifact.

Design is the most appropriate organizing principle. Design puts the emphasis on invention of an artifact by the faculty, those who will have the responsibility for bringing it into action. The artifact is not immutable or perfect but offers that balanced arrangement of resources, abilities, and interests that promises educational effectiveness.

The underlying assumption guiding curricular change is that organizations and cultures gravitate against innovation. Innovative organizations must be consciously designed. They do not simply evolve. Of consequence, organizational participants must develop strategies geared toward ongoing initiatives and assessment.

Organizational leaders are catalysts for change rather than producers of physical change. Change is not causal, linear, or predictable, and it has complex, often spontaneous, ramifications. Given these assumptions, the work of managing curricular change is more dynamic than static, more an art of interpreting one's environment and culture than a science of developing effective managerial practices. Developing curricular change is as much a process as a goal. The point, then, is to suggest a philosophy that offers individuals ways to think about how to act in their own organizations as they struggle to invent and implement curricular innovations.

REFERENCES

The Educational Resources Information Center (ERIC) Clearinghouse on Higher Education abstracts and indexes the current literature on higher education for inclusion in ERIC's data base and announcement in ERIC's monthly bibliographic journal, *Resources in Education* (RIE). Most of these publications are available through the ERIC Document Reproduction Service (EDRS). For publications cited in this bibliography that are available from EDRS, ordering number and price code are included. Readers who wish to order a publication should write to the ERIC Document Reproduction Service, 7420 Fullerton Rd., Suite 110, Springfield, VA 22153-2852. (Phone orders with VISA or MasterCard are taken at 800-443-ERIC or 703-440-1400.) When ordering, please specify the document (ED) number. Documents are available as noted in microfiche (MF) and paper copy (PC). If you have the price code ready when you call EDRS, an exact price can be quoted. The last page of the latest issue of *Resources in Education* also has the current cost, listed by code.

Aiken, S.H., K. Anderson, M. Dinnerstein, J. Lensink, and P. MacCorquodale. 1987. "Trying Transformations: Curriculum Integration and the Problem of Resistance." *Signs* 12(2): 255–75.

Alexander, C. 1964. *Notes on the Synthesis of Form.* Cambridge, Mass: Harvard Univ. Press.

Alpert, R.M. 1980. "Professionalism and Educational Reform: The Case of Hampshire College. *Journal of Higher Education* 51(5): 497–518.

Altbach, P.G. 1987. "Review Symposium: Involvement in Learning." *Higher Education* 14: 461–71.

American Association of State Colleges and Universities. 1986. *Defining and Assessing Baccalaureate Skills: Ten Case Studies.* Washington, D.C.: Author. ED 293 379. 31 pp. MF–01; PC–02.

American Council on Education. 1984. *Fact Book on Higher Education.* New York: ACE/Macmillan.

Andersen, M.L. 1988. "Changing the Curriculum in Higher Education." In *Reconstructing the Academy: Women's Education and Women's Studies,* edited by E. Minnich, J. O'Barr, and R. Rosenfeld. Chicago: Univ. of Chicago Press.

Apple, M.W. 1983. "Curriculum in 2000: Tensions and Possibilities." *Educational Digest* 49: 2–6.

Argyris, C., and D.A. Schon. 1978. *Organizational Learning.* Reading, Mass.: Addison-Wesley.

Association of American Colleges. 1986. *Integrity in the College Curriculum.* Washington, D.C.: Author.

Azaroff, L.V. 1982. "Industry/University Collaboration." *Research Management* 25(3): 31–34.

Babin, P. Fall 1979. "A Curriculum Orientation Profile." *Education Canada:* 38–42.

Banham, R. 1974. *The Aspen Papers.* New York: Praeger.

Banta, T. 1988. *Implementing Outcomes Assessment.* New Directions for Institutional Research No. 59. San Francisco: Jossey-Bass.

Barnard, J. 1981. "Women's Educational Needs." In *The Modern American College.* edited by A. Chickering. San Francisco: Jossey-Bass.

Barzun, J. 1959. *The House of Intellect.* New York: Harper Torchbook.

Bell, D. 1966. *The Reforming of General Education.* New York: Columbia Univ. Press.

Ben David, J. 1972. *American Higher Education.* New York: McGraw-Hill.

———. 1977. *Centers of Learning.* New York: McGraw-Hill.

Benjamin, E. 1985. "Expanding the Context of Curricular Reform." *Academe* 71(5): 22–25.

Bennett, J.B. 1983. *Managing the Academic Department.* New York: ACE/Macmillan.

Bennett, J.B., and D.S. Figuli. 1990. *Enhancing Departmental Leadership.* New York: Ace/Macmillan.

Bennett, W. 1984. *To Reclaim a Legacy.* Washington, D.C.: National Endowment for the Humanities.

Bergquist, W., R. Gould, and E. Greenberg. 1981. *Designing Undergraduate Education.* San Francisco: Jossey-Bass.

Bergquist, W., and S. Phillips. 1977. *A Handbook for Faculty Development.* Washington, D.C.: Council for the Advancement of Small Colleges.

Bernsen, J. 1982. *Design: The Problem Comes First.* Copenhagen: Danish Design Council.

Berstein, B. 1977. *Class, Codes, and Control.* Vol. 3. London: Routledge & Kegan Paul.

Beyer, L.E., and M.W. Apple. 1988. *The Curriculum: Problems, Politics, and Possibilities.* Albany: State Univ. of New York Press.

Birnbaum, R. 1988. *How Colleges Work.* San Francisco: Jossey-Bass.

Blau, P. 1973. *The Organization of Academic Work.* New York: John Wiley & Sons.

Bloom, A. 1987. *The Closing of the American Mind.* New York: Simon & Schuster.

Bloom, B. 1956. *Taxonomy of Educational Objectives.* Handbook 1, *The Cognitive Domain.* New York: David McKay Co.

Bok, D. 1982. *Beyond the Ivory Tower: Social Responsibilities of the Modern University.* Cambridge, Mass.: Harvard Univ. Press.

———. 1986. *Higher Learning.* Cambridge, Mass.: Harvard Univ. Press.

Bourdieu, P., and J. Passeron. 1977. *Reproduction in Education, Society, and Culture.* Beverly Hills, Cal.: Sage.

Bowen, H.R. 1977. *Investment in Learning.* San Francisco: Jossey-Bass.

Bowen, H.R., and J.H. Schuster. 1986. *American Professors.* New York: Oxford Univ. Press.

Bowles, S., and H. Gintis. 1976. *Schooling in Capitalist America*. New York: Basic Books.

Boyer, E. 1987. *College: The Undergraduate Experience in America*. New York: Harper & Row.

Boyer, E.L., and A. Levine. 1981. *A Quest for Common Learning*. Washington, D.C.: Carnegie Foundation.

Brentlinger, W.B. 1986. "Curricula for the Twenty-first Century." Paper presented at the Regional Conference on University Teaching, Las Cruces, New Mexico.

Brockliss, L. 1987. *French Higher Education in the 17th and 18th Centuries: A Cultural History*. Oxford, Eng.: Clarendon Press.

Broudy, H.S. 1977. "Can Curriculum Escape the Disciplines?" In *Curriculum Handbook*, edited by L. Rubin. Boston: Allyn & Bacon.

Brunschwig, F., and R. Breslin. 1982. "Scientific and Technical Literacy: A Major Innovation and Challenge."

Caws, P. 1974. "Instruction and Inquiry." *Daedalus* 103(4): 18–24.

CERI/OECD. 1972. *Interdisciplinarity: Problems of Teaching and Research in Universities*. Paris: Author.

Chaffee, E.E. 1983. *Rational Decision Making in Higher Education*. Boulder, Colo.: NCHEMS.

———. 1989. *Strategy and Effectiveness in Systems of Higher Education*. Vol. 5. In *Higher Education: Handbook of Theory and Research*, edited by J. Smart. New York: Agathon Press.

Chaffee, E.E., and W. Tierney. 1988. *Collegiate Culture and Leadership Strategies*. New York: ACE/Macmillan.

Cherryholmes, C. 1988. *Power and Criticism*. New York: Teachers College Press.

Chickering, A. 1981. *The Modern American College*. San Francisco: Jossey-Bass.

Chickering, A., and Z. Gamson. 1987. "Seven Principles for Good Practice. *AAHE Bulletin*: 3–6.

Chickering, A., D. Halliburton, W. Berguist, and J. Lindquist. 1977. *Developing the College Curriculum*. Washington, D.C.: Council for the Advancement of Small Colleges. ED 152 125. 307 pp. MF–01; PC–13.

Christensen, J.L., and E.R. Johnston. 1987. "The Finite Optometric Curriculum." *Journal of Optometric Education* 13(2): 73–76.

Clark, B.R. 1970. *The Distinctive College: Antioch, Reed, and Swarthmore*. Chicago: Aldine.

———. 1983. *The Higher Education System: Academic Organization in Cross-National Perspective*. Berkeley: Univ. of California Press.

———. 1987. *The Academic Life: Small Worlds, Different Worlds*. Princeton, N.J.: Princeton Univ. Press.

Clark, M.E., and S.A. Wawrytko. 1990. *Rethinking the Curriculum: Toward an Integrated, Interdisciplinary College Education*. New York: Greenwood Press.

Cohen, A.M., et al. 1986. *Key Resources on Community Colleges*. San

Francisco: Jossey-Bass.

Cohen, M.D., and J.G. March. 1974. *Leadership and Ambiguity.* New York: McGraw-Hill.

Cohen, P.A. 1983. "Computing at Dartmouth: Survey of Faculty and Students." *Journal of Educational Technical Systems* 12(1): 95–106.

Conrad, C.F. 1978. *The Undergraduate Curriculum: A Guide to Innovation and Reform.* Boulder, Colo.: Westview Press.

———. 1985a. *Access to Quality Undergraduate Education.* Atlanta: Southern Regional Education Board, Commission for Educational Quality. ED 260 662. 19 pp. MF–01; PC–01.

———. 1985b. *ASHE Reader on Academic Programs in Colleges and Universities.* Lexington, Mass.: Ginn & Co.

Conrad, C.F., and R.T. Blackburn. 1985. *Program Quality in Higher Education: A Review and Critique of Literature and Research.* Vol. 1. In *Higher Education: Handbook of Theory and Research,* edited by J. Smart. New York: Agathon Press.

Conrad, C.F., and J.G. Haworth. 1991. "Liberating Education in the Modern Metropolitan University." *Metropolitan University* 2(2): 21.

Conrad, C.F., and A. Pratt. 1983. "Making Decisions about the Curriculum: From Metaphor to Model." *Journal of Higher Education* 54(5): 16–30.

Conrad, C.F., and J.C. Wyer. 1980. *Liberal Education in Transition.* AAHE-ERIC Higher Education Report No. 3. Washington, D.C.: American Association for Higher Education. ED 188 539. 73 pp. MF–01; PC–03.

Crane, W. 1977. *The Bases of Design.* Reprint. London: George Bell.

Cross, K.P., and A.-M. McCartan. 1984. *Adult Learning: State Policies and Institutional Practice.* ASHE-ERIC Higher Education Report No. 1. Washington, D.C.: Association for the Study of Higher Education. ED 246 831. 162 pp. MF–01; PC–07.

Cullen, J.B. 1978. *The Structure of Professionalism.* New York: Petrocelli Books.

Daft, R., and S. Becker. 1978. "Revising the Theory: Garbage Cans, Idea Champions, and Innovations." In *The Innovative Organization.* New York: Elsevier.

DeBono, E. 1984. "Critical Thinking Is not Enough." *Educational Leadership* 42: 16–17.

Diamond, R.M. 1989. *Designing and Improving Courses and Curricula in Higher Education: A Systematic Approach.* San Francisco: Jossey-Bass.

Dill, D., and C. Friedman. 1979. "An Analysis of Framework for Research on Innovation and Change in Higher Education." *Review of Educational Research* 49: 411–35.

Doll, W.E., Jr. 1989. "Foundations for a Postmodern Curriculum." *Journal of Curriculum Studies* 21(3): 243–53.

Donald, J.G. 1986. "Knowledge and the University Curriculum." *Higher Education* 15: 267–82.

Dressel, P. 1971. *College and University Curriculum*. Berkeley, Cal.: McCutchan.

D'Souza, D. 1991. *Illiberal Education: The Politics of Race and Sex on Campus*. New York: Free Press.

Dubin, R., and T.C. Taveggia. 1968. *The Teaching-Learning Paradox*. Eugene: Univ. of Oregon, Center for Advanced Study of Educational Administration.

Eberle, W.D. 1974. "What Business Expects of Higher Education." *Liberal Education* 60(1): 5–14.

Eble, K.E. 1983. *The Aims of College Teaching*. San Francisco: Jossey-Bass.

Ehrle, E.E., and J.B. Bennett. 1988. *Managing the Academic Enterprise*. New York: ACE/Macmillan.

Eisner, E., and E. Vallance. 1974. *Conflicting Conceptions of Curriculum*. Berkeley, Cal.: McCutchan.

El-Khawas, E. 1987. *Campus Trends 1987*. Washington, D.C.: American Council on Education.

Emerson, S. 1957. *Design: A Creative Approach*. Scranton, Pa.: International Textbook Co.

Enarson, H.L. 1987. "The Undergraduate Curriculum: Who's In Charge?" *NASULGC Newsletter*. Toledo, Ohio: Toledo Univ.

English, F.W. 1980. "Curriculum Mapping." *Educational Leadership* 37: 558–59.

Ewell, P. 1984. *Using Student Outcomes Information in Program Planning and Decision Making*. Report to the Kellogg Foundation. Boulder, Colo.: NCHEMS.

———. 1985. "Assessment: What's It All About?" *Change* 17(6): 32–36.

Fairweather, J. 1988. *Entrepreneurship and Higher Education: Lessons for Colleges, Universities, and Industry*. ASHE-ERIC Higher Education Report No. 6. Washington, D.C.: Association for the Study of Higher Education. ED 307 841. 137 pp. MF–01; PC–06.

Farnham, C., ed. 1987. *The Impact of Feminist Research on the Academy*. Bloomington: Indiana Univ. Press.

Ferguson, C.C. 1981. "Inside-out Curriculum." *Educational Leadership* 39: 114–16.

Fincher, C. 1986. *Trends and Issues in Curriculum Development*. Vol. 2. In *Higher Education: Handbook of Theory and Research*, edited by J. Smart. New York: Agathon.

Finn, C.E. 1982. "A Call for Quality Education." *American Education* 18(1): 31–36.

Firestone, W., and H. Corbett. 1988. "Planned Organizational Change." In *Handbook of Research on Educational Change*. White Plains, N.Y.: Longman.

Firestone, W., H. Corbett, and G. Rossman. 1987. "Resistance to Planned Change and the Sacred School Structure." *Educational Administration Quarterly* 23(4): 36–59.

Foshay, A.W., ed. 1970. *The Professional as Educator*. New York:

Columbia Univ., Teachers College Press.

Franklin, P. 1988. "The Prospects for General Education in American Higher Education." In *Cultural Literacy and the Idea of General Education*. NSSE 87th Yearbook. Chicago: Univ. of Chicago Press.

Freire, P. 1970. *Pedagogy of the Oppressed*. Hammondsworth, Eng.: Penguin Books.

Gaff, J. 1975. *Toward Faculty Renewal*. San Francisco: Jossey-Bass.

———. 1983. *General Education Today*. San Francisco: Jossey-Bass.

Galbraith, J.K. 1982. "Designing the Innovative Organization." *Organizational Dynamics* 10: 5–25.

———. 1987. "On Teaching a Fractured Macroeconomics." *Journal of Economic Education* 18(2): 213–26.

Gamson, Z., et al. 1984. *Liberating Education*. San Francisco: Jossey-Bass.

Giroux, H.A. 1983. *Theory and Resistance in Education*. South Hadley, Mass.: Bergin & Garvey.

Giroux, H.A., and R. Simon. 1984. "Curriculum Study and Cultural Politics." *Journal of Education* 166: 226–38.

Glaser, R. 1968. "Ten Untenable Assumptions." *Educational Record* 49: 140–59.

Glazer, N. 1987. "Questioning Eclectic Practice in Curriculum Change: A Marxist Perspective." *Signs* 12(2): 293–304.

Goodman, D.M. 1982. "Making Liberal Education Work in a Technological Culture." *Liberal Education* 68: 63–68.

Gould, J.W. 1964. "The Academic Deanship." In *The Academic Deanship in American Colleges and Universities*, edited by A. Dibden. Carbondale: Southern Illinois Univ. Press.

Grant, G., and D. Riesman. 1978. *The Perpetual Dream: Reform and Experiment in the American College*. Chicago: Univ. of Chicago Press.

Gregory, M., and D. Wanda. 1987. "Business Education for a Changing World." In *National Business Education Yearbook* No. 25. Reston, Va.: National Business Education Association.

Grumet, M. 1983. "Curriculum as Theatre: Merely Players." *Curriculum Inquiry* 8(1): 37–64.

Gumport, P. 1988. "Curricula as Signposts of Cultural Change." *Review of Higher Education* 12(1): 49–61.

Haigh, R.W. 1985. "Planning for Computer Literacy." *Journal of Higher Education* 56: 161–71.

Hall, J.W., and B.L. Keules. 1982. *In Opposition to Core Curriculum: Alternative Models for Undergraduate Education*. Westport, Conn.: Greenwood Press.

Harris, J. 1987. *Assessment: Providing Quality Assurance for Students, Programs, and Career Guidance*. New Directions for Higher Education No. 57. San Francisco: Jossey-Bass.

Hefferlin, J.B. 1969. *The Dynamics of Academic Reform*. San Francisco: Jossey-Bass.

Herbert, T. 1976. *Dimensions of Organizational Behavior*. New York: Macmillan.

Hirst, P. 1974. *Knowledge and the Curriculum*. Boston: Routledge & Kegan Paul.

Hoffnung, M. 1984. "Feminist Transformation: Teaching Experimental Psychology." Working paper 140. Wellesley, Mass.: Wellesley College, Center for Research on Women.

Hofstadter, R., and W. Smith. 1961. "Inaugural Address [1869] of C.W. Eliot." In *American Higher Education: A Documentary History*, vol. 2. Chicago: Univ. of Chicago Press.

Holland, J.R. 1985. "A Nation at Risk." *Review of Higher Education* 9(1): 51–65.

Hopmann, S. 1991. "The Multiple Realities of Curriculum Policy Making." Paper presented at an annual meeting of AERA, April, Chicago, Illinois. ED 023 291. 22 pp. MF–01; PC–01.

Houle, C.O. 1980. *Continuing Learning in the Professions*. San Francisco: Jossey-Bass.

Illich, I. 1971. *Deschooling Society*. New York: Harper & Row.

Jones, R.M. 1981. *Experiment at Evergreen*. Cambridge, Mass.: Schenkman Books.

Kadish, M. 1991. *Toward an Ethic of Higher Education*. Stanford, Cal.: Stanford Univ. Press.

Kagan, R.L. 1975. "Universities in Castille, 1500–1810. In *The University in Society*, vol. 2, edited by L. Stone. Princeton, N.J.: Princeton Univ. Press.

Kerr, C., and M. Gade. 1987. "The Contemporary College President." *American Scholar*: 29–44.

Kidder, T. 1987. "Agenda for the 21st Century." *Christian Science Monitor*.

King, J.B. 1986. "Three Faces of Thinking." *Journal of Higher Education* 57: 78–92.

Klein, G.A. 1983. "Curriculum Development vs. Education." *Teaching College Record* 84: 821–36.

LaFauci, H.M. 1970. *Team Teaching at the College Level*. New York: Pergamon Press.

Lee, B.A. 1985. "Faculty Involvement in Enhancing Student Learning." *Academe* 71(5): 22–25.

Levine, A. 1980. *Why Innovation Fails*. Albany: State Univ. of New York Press.

———. 1981. *Handbook on the Undergraduate Curriculum*. San Francisco: Jossey-Bass.

Levine, A., and J. Weingart. 1973. *Reform of Undergraduate Education*. San Francisco: Jossey-Bass.

Li Bao Ming. 1991. "Collegiate Curricula in China: Stability and Change under a Centralized System." Doctoral dissertation, Penn State Univ.

Lieberman, M.B. 1956. *Education as a Profession*. Englewood Cliffs,

N.J.: Prentice-Hall.

Light, D.L. 1979. "Surface Data and Deep Structure." *Administrative Science Quarterly* 24(4): 551–59.

Lindquist, J. 1978. *Strategies for Change*. Berkeley, Cal.: Pacific Soundings Press.

Lynton, E.A. 1981. "A Role for Colleges in Corporate Training and Development." In *Partnerships with Business and the Professions,* edited by E.A. Lynton. Washington, D.C.: American Association for Higher Education.

Lynton, E.A., and S.E. Elman. 1987. *New Priorities for the University*. San Francisco: Jossey-Bass.

McCutcheon, G. 1982. "What in the World Is Curriculum Theory?" *Theory and Practice* 21: 18–22.

McHenry, D.E. 1977. *Academic Departments*. San Francisco: Jossey-Bass.

McIntosh, P. 1983. "Interactive Phases of Curricular Revision: A Feminist Perspective." Working paper 124. Wellesley, Mass.: Wellesley College.

McKelvie, B.D. 1986. "The University's Statement of Goals." *Higher Education* 15: 151–63.

McLeod, S.H., ed. 1988. *Strengthening Programs for Writing across the Curriculum*. New Directions for Teaching and Learning No. 36. San Francisco: Jossey-Bass.

Marsden, W.E. 1989. "All in a Good Cause." *Journal of Curriculum Studies* 21(6): 509–26.

Marsh, P.T., ed. 1988. *Contesting the Boundaries of Liberal and Professional Education*. New York: Syracuse Univ. Press.

Martin, W.B. 1983. "Education for Character, Career, and Society." *Change* 15: 35–42.

Martorana, S.V., and E. Kuhns. 1975. *Managing Academic Change*. San Francisco: Jossey-Bass.

May, H.F. 1976. *The Enlightenment in America*. New York: Oxford Univ. Press.

Mayhew, L.B., and P.J. Ford. 1971. *Changing the Curriculum*. San Francisco: Jossey-Bass.

Meister, J.S. 1982. "Sociologist Looks at Two Schools: The Amherst and Hampshire Eperience." *Change* 14: 26–34.

Menges, R.J., and B.C. Mathis. 1988. *Key Resources on Teaching, Learning, Curriculum, and Faculty Development*. San Francisco: Jossey-Bass.

Meyers, C. 1986. *Teaching Students to Think Critically*. San Francisco: Jossey-Bass.

Millar, C., T. Morphet, and T. Saddington. 1986. "Curriculum Negotiation in Professional Adult Education." *Journal of Curriculum Studies* 18(4): 429–43.

Minnich, E., J. O'Barr, and R. Rosenfeld, eds. 1988. *Reconstructing the Academy: Women's Education and Women's Studies*. Chicago:

Univ. of Chicago Press.

Molinari, J. 1982. "Environmental Studies at the Undergraduate Level: Curriculum and the Integration of Knowledge." Doctoral dissertation, Penn State Univ.

Mooney, C.J. 1988. "Sweeping Curricular Change Is Under Way at Stanford." *Chronicle of Higher Education* 35: 14.

Mortimer, K.P. 1984. *Involvement in Learning.* Washington, D.C.: National Institute of Education. ED 246 833. 127 pp. MF–01; PC–06.

Mortimer, K.P., and T.R. McConnell. 1978. *Sharing Authority Effectively.* San Francisco: Jossey-Bass.

Muscatine, C. 1985. "Faculty Responsibility for the Curriculum." *Academe* 71(5): 18–21.

Naisbitt, J. 1982. *Megatrends.* New York: Warner Books.

Naisbitt, J., and P. Aburdene. 1990. *Megatrends 2000.* New York: Morrow.

National Center for Education Statistics. 1989. *The Condition of Education, 1975–1989.* Washington, D.C.: U.S. Dept. of Education.

National Governors Association, Task Force on College Quality. 1986. *Time for Results.* Washington, D.C.: Center for Policy Research and Analysis. ED 279 609. 99 pp. MF–01; PC not available EDRS.

Nemerowicz, G., and E. Rosi. Summer 1990. "Education for Leadership and Social Responsibility." *Perspectives:* 21–30.

Newman, F. 1985. *Higher Education and American Resurgence.* New York: Carnegie Foundation.

Office of Educational Research and Improvement. 1988. *Education Indicator.* Washington, D.C.: U.S. Dept. of Education.

Ornstein, R., and P. Ehrlich. 1989. *New World, New Mind: Moving toward Conscious Evolution.* New York: Simon & Schuster.

Oxford University. 1971. *The Compact Edition of the Oxford English Dictionary.* Oxford Univ. Press.

Pace, C.R. 1979. *Measuring Outcomes of College.* San Francisco: Jossey-Bass.

Parsons, T. 1970. "The Professional as Educator." In *The Professional as Educator,* edited by A.W. Foshay. New York: Columbia Univ., Teachers College Press.

Pascarella, E., and P.T. Terenzini. 1991. *How College Affects Students.* San Francisco: Jossey-Bass.

Patterson, F., and C. Longworth. 1966. *The Making of a College.* Cambridge, Mass.: MIT Press.

Pazandak, C.H. 1989. *Improving Undergraduate Education in Large Universities.* New Directions in Higher Education No. 66. San Francisco: Jossey-Bass.

Peterson, M., and L. Metz. 1988. *Key Resources on Higher Education Governance, Management, and Leadership.* San Francisco: Jossey-Bass.

Phenix, P.H. 1964. *Realms of Meaning.* New York: McGraw-Hill.

Popkewitz, T.S. 1988. "Knowledge, Power: A General Curriculum." In *Cultural Literacy and the Idea of General Education*. NSSE 87th Yearbook. Chicago: Univ. of Chicago Press.

Popkewitz, T.S., A. Pitman, and A. Barry. "Educational Reform and Its Millennial Quality: The 1980s." *Journal of Curriculum Studies* 18(3): 267–83.

Ratcliff, J.L., and D. Vandeharr. 1987. "The Effect of New Technologies on the Curriculum of Colleges and Universities." Paper presented at an annual meeting of the American Educational Research Association.

Reid, W. 1986. "Curriculum Theory and Curriculum Change." *Journal of Curriculum Studies* 18(2): 151–63.

Riesman, D. 1956. *Constraint and Variety in American Education*. New York: Doubleday-Anchor.

Rossides, D.W. 1987. "Knee-jerk Formalism." *Journal of Higher Education* 58(4): 404–29.

Rothblatt, S. 1988. "General Education on the American Campus." In *Cultural Literacy and the Idea of General Education*. NSSE 87th Yearbook. Chicago: Univ. of Chicago Press.

Rudolph, F. 1977. *Curriculum*. San Francisco: Jossey-Bass.

———. 1984. "The Power of Professors: The Impact of Specialization and Professionalization on the Curriculum." *Change* 16: 12–17.

Sanford, N. 1962. *The American College*. New York: John Wiley & Sons.

Schubert, W. 1980. *Curriculum Books: The First Eighty Years*. Washington, D.C.: University Press of America.

———. 1986. *Curriculum: Perspective, Paradigm, and Possibility*. New York: Macmillan.

Schuster, J.H., D.W. Wheeler, et al. 1990. *Enhancing Faculty Careers*. San Francisco: Jossey-Bass.

Schuster, M., and S. Van Dyne. 1984. "Placing Women in the Liberal Arts: Stages of Curriculum Transformation." *Harvard Educational Review* 54: 413–28.

———. 1985. *Women's Place in the Academy*. Towota, N.J.: Rowman & Allanheld.

Schwab, J.J. 1969. "The Practical: A Language for Curriculum." *School Review* 78: 1–23.

Scott, R.A. 1981. "Curriculum as Covenant." *College Board Review* 121: 20–31.

Seymour, D.T. 1988. *Developing Academic Programs: The Climate for Innovation*. ASHE-ERIC Higher Education Report No. 3. Washington, D.C.: Association for the Study of Higher Education. ED 305 015. 148 pp. MF–01; PC–06.

Shadower, M.J. 1987. "The Small Department: Curriculum in Transition." Paper presented at an annual meeting of the Speech Communications Association, Boston, Massachusetts. ED 288 224. 12 pp. MF–01; PC–01.

Shils, E. 1983. *The Academic Ethic.* Chicago: Univ. of Chicago Press.

Simon, H.F. 1969. *The Sciences of the Artificial.* Cambridge, Mass.: MIT Press.

Sloan, D. 1971. "Harmony, Chaos, and Consensus: The American College Curriculum." *Teachers College Record* 73(2): 221.

Smith, P. 1990. *Killing the Spirit.* New York: Viking Press.

Smuckler, R., and L. Sommers. Fall 1988. "Internationalizing the Curriculum." National Forum. *Phi Kappa Phi Journal:* 5–10.

Smutz, W.D. 1984. "Formal Boundary Spanners and Organizational Change." Doctoral dissertation, Penn State Univ.

Squires, G. 1987. *The Curriculum beyond High School.* London: Hodder & Stougton.

———. 1990. *First Degree: The Undergraduate Curriculum.* Buckingham, Eng.: Society for Research into Higher Education. ED 326 168. 184 pp. MF–01; PC–08.

Stark, J.S., and M.A. Lowther. 1986. *Designing the Learning Plan: A Review of Research and Theory Related to College Curricula.* Ann Arbor: Regents of the Univ. of Michigan.

Stark, J.S., et al. 1988. *Reflections on Course Planning.* Technical Report 88-C-002.2. Ann Arbor: Regents of the Univ. of Michigan.

Stone, L. 1974. *The University in Society.* 2 vols. Princeton, N.J.: Princeton Univ. Press.

Sutcliffe, H. 1982. "A Comparison of the Teaching of Chemistry in French Grandes Ecoles and British Universities." *Studies in Higher Education* 7(1): 57–64.

Taylor, H. 1950. *Essays in Teaching.* New York: Harper.

Tellefsen, T.E. 1990. *Improving College Management: An Integrated Systems Approach.* San Francisco: Jossey-Bass.

Tierney, W.G. 1988a. "Organizational Culture in Higher Education: Defining the Essentials." *Journal of Higher Education:* 59(1): 2–21.

———. 1988b. *The Web of Leadership: The Presidency in Higher Education.* Greenwich, Conn.: JAI Press.

———. 1989a. "Cultural Politics and the Curriculum in Postsecondary Education." *Journal of Education:* 171(3): 72–88.

———. 1989b. *Curricular Landscapes, Democratic Vistas: Transformative Leadership in Higher Education.* New York: Praeger.

———. 1991a. "Academic Work and Institutional Culture: Constructing Knowledge." *Review of Higher Education* 14(2): 201–219.

———, ed. 1991b. *Culture and Ideology in Higher Education: Advancing a Critical Agenda.* New York: Praeger.

Toombs, W., and M. Escala. 1986. "Doing the Right Thing: Problems of Academic Organization." Paper presented at an annual conference of the Association for the Study of Higher Education, Washington, D.C. ED 281 441. 34 pp. MF–01; PC–02.

Toombs, W., J. Fairweather, et al. August 1989. "Open to View: Practice and Purpose in General Education." Report to the Exxon Education Foundation.

Trimbur, J. Summer 1986. "To Reclaim a Legacy: Cultural Literacy and the Discourse of Crisis." *Liberal Education* 72: 109–19.

Tuchman, B.W. 1978. *A Distant Mirror: The Calamitous 14th Century.* New York: Alfred A. Knopf.

Tucker, A. 1984. *Chairing the Academic Department.* Washington, D.C.: American Council on Education.

Tucker, A., and R.A. Bryan. 1988. *The Academic Dean.* New York: ACE/Mac-Millan.

Turmears, W.A. 1982. "Engineering Degree Curricula for the Future. *Higher Education* 11: 397–403.

Tyler, R. 1950. *Basic Principles of Curriculum and Instruction.* Chicago: Univ. of Chicago Press.

Uwalaka, O. 1986. "Organizational Factors Related to Professional Developmental Practices for Faculty." Doctoral dissertation. Penn State Univ.

Veblen, T. 1957. *Higher Learning in America.* New York: Hill & Wang.

Veysey, L. 1973. "Stability and Experiment." In *Content and Context*, edited by K. Kaysen. New York: McGraw-Hill.

Vollmer, H.M., and D.L. Mills. 1966. *Professionalization.* Englewood Cliffs, N.J.: Prentice-Hall.

Waltzer, H. 1983. "In Defense of Academic Departments: Providing for the Development, Preservation, and Transmission of Knowledge." *Change* 15: 16–20.

Walzer, J.B. 1982. "New Knowledge or a New Discipline? Women's Studies at the University." *Change* 14: 21–23.

Weaver, F.S. 1981. "Academic Disciplines and Undergraduate Liberal Arts Education." *Liberal Education* 67: 151–165.

Weingartner, R.H. 1979. "Northwestern and Reform of the Undergraduate Curriculum." *Liberal Education* 65: 323-32.

Wentzel, P. 1986. "Approved Athletic Training Programs and the National Certification Exam: A Comparative Study of Performance and Curriculums." Doctoral dissertation. Penn State Univ.

Wharton, C.R. 1979. "New Dimensions of Basic Learning." *Change* 11: 38–41.

White, A., ed. 1981. *Interdisciplinary Teaching.* New Directions in Teaching and Learning No. 8. San Francisco: Jossey-Bass.

White, E. 1989. *Developing Successful College Writing Programs.* San Francisco: Jossey-Bass.

Williams, R. 1986. *Rethinking Education: The Coming Age of Enlightenment.*

Wood, L., and B. Davis. 1978. *Designing and Evaluating Higher Education Curricula.* ASHE-ERIC Higher Education Report No. 8. Washington, D.C.: Association for the Study of Higher Education. ED 165 669. 72 pp. MF–01; PC–03.

Zavarzadeh, M., and D. Morton. October/November 1987. "War of Words: The Battle of (and for) English." *In These Times:* 18–19.

Zemsky, R. 1989 *Structure and Coherence; Measuring the Under-graduate Curriculum*. Washington, D.C.: Association of American Colleges. ED 310 658. 47 pp. MF–01; PC not available EDRS.

INDEX

A

Academic administrators, 82
Academic freedom, 51
Academic practice
    dilemmas, 52
Academic Program Evaluation Project, 59
Action plans, 67
Administrators
    role in curriculum development, 39
Alternative theorists, 43, 44
American Association of State Colleges and Universities, 59, 69
American Association of University Professors, 51, 53
American Council on Education, 53, 66
Analysis of curriculum, 57
Artificial world, 19
Association of Governing Boards, 53
Assumptions of curricular theory, 42

B

Baseline data
    students, 84
Black studies, 57
Boundary setting, 13
Butler, Nicholas Murray, 41

C

Career based curriculum, 46
Carnegie Foundation, 8, 66
Certification, 33
Challenges and the curriculum, 5
Challenges of curricular change, 57
Change agent, 78
Closing of the American Mind, 35
Co-curricular activities, 36
Colonial universities
    America, 14
Common body of knowledge theory, 42
Common Sense, 14
Comparative data, 66
Competency based curriculum, 46
Constellations, 32
Control of courses, 29
Core courses, 36
Courses
    information, 29
    clusters, 32
    patterns, 30
    review, 30

Fear of the unknown, 76
Feminist studies, 43
FOCUS project, 59
Functional approach to curriculum design, 25
Future based curriculum, 46

G

Glasgow, University of, 13

H

Hampshire College, 47
Heritage based curriculum, 46
Higher education, principal mandate, 6
Hutchins, Robert Maynard, 41

I

Idea champions, 73, 74, 80
Idea development, 81
Incentives for change, 73, 79, 80
Inertia, organizational, 76
Innovative organizations, 79
Institutional mission, 83
Instructional system, 17
Integrated learning, 8
Intellectual accountability, 9, 10
Invisible paradigms, 44

K

Kenyon College catalog, 1

L

Learning
        costs, 6
        structure, 30
Legitimation of curricular transformation, 60, 61
Legitimation of the topic, 62, 63

M

Major fields, 5
Managing academic change, 71, 74
Medieval universities, 13
        France, 13
        Germany, 13
        Scotland, 13
        Spain, 13
Minnesota, University of, 59
Monmouth College, 64

N

National Defense Education Act, 31
Negotiation, 67
Normative data, 66
Nova University, 5

O

Obstacles to professionalization, 51
Office of Educational Research and Improvement, 66
Organizational change, 67
      planning, 71
Organizational
      leaders, 80
      options, 6
      processes, 73
      stability, 79
Organizations
      culture, 76
      framework of change, 73
      structures and roles, 73
      theoretical perspectives, 72

P

Penn State University, 66
Pennsylvania, University of, 66
Plan for learning, 17
Political perspective
      organizations, 72
Position papers, 67
Postsecondary system
      differentiation, 5
      expansion, 5
Professional practice, 49
Professionalization, 50, 54
Professions, 49
Program review, 33, 65

R

Reconceptualization of curriculum, 41
Reform strategy, 82
Resistance to innovation, 75-77
Retrospection, 69

S

Schema of change, 78
Science
      natural systems, 19

ASHE-ERIC HIGHER EDUCATION REPORTS

Since 1983, the Association for the Study of Higher Education (ASHE) and the Educational Resources Information Center (ERIC) Clearinghouse on Higher Education, a sponsored project of the School of Education and Human Development at The George Washington University, have cosponsored the *ASHE-ERIC Higher Education Report* series. The 1991 series is the twentieth overall and the third to be published by the School of Education and Human Development at the George Washington University.

Each monograph is the definitive analysis of a tough higher education problem, based on thorough research of pertinent literature and institutional experiences. Topics are identified by a national survey. Noted practitioners and scholars are then commissioned to write the reports, with experts providing critical reviews of each manuscript before publication.

Eight monographs (10 before 1985) in the ASHE-ERIC Higher Education Report series are published each year and are available on individual and subscription bases. Subscription to eight issues is $90.00 annually; $70 to members of AAHE, AIR, or AERA; and $60 to ASHE members. All foreign subscribers must include an additional $10 per series year for postage.

To order single copies of existing reports, use the order form on the last page of this book. Regular prices, and special rates available to members of AAHE, AIR, AERA and ASHE, are as follows:

Series	Regular	Members
1990 and 91	$17.00	$12.75
1988 and 89	15.00	11.25
1985 to 87	10.00	7.50
1983 and 84	7.50	6.00
before 1983	6.50	5.00

Price includes book rate postage within the U.S. For foreign orders, please add $1.00 per book. Fast United Parcel Service available within the contiguous U.S. at $2.50 for each order under $50.00, and calculated at 5% of invoice total for orders $50.00 or above.

All orders under $45.00 must be prepaid. Make check payable to ASHE-ERIC. For Visa or MasterCard, include card number, expiration date and signature. A bulk discount of 10% is available on orders of 10 or more books, and 40% on orders of 25 or more books (not applicable on subscriptions).

Address order to
  ASHE-ERIC Higher Education Reports
  The George Washington University
  1 Dupont Circle, Suite 630
  Washington, DC 20036
Or phone (202) 296-2597
  Write or call for a complete catalog.

1991 ASHE-ERIC Higher Education Reports

1. Active Learning: Creating Excitement in the Classroom
   Charles C. Bonwell and James A. Eison

2. Realizing Gender Equality in Higher Education: The Need to Integrate Work/Family Issues
   Nancy Hensel

3. Academic Advising for Student Success: A System of Shared Responsibility
   by Susan H. Frost

4. Cooperative Learning: Increasing College Faculty Instructional Productivity
   by David W. Johnson, Roger T. Johnson, and Karl A. Smith

5. High School–College Partnerships: Conceptual Models, Programs, and Issues
   by Arthur Richard Greenberg

1990 ASHE-ERIC Higher Education Reports

1. The Campus Green: Fund Raising in Higher Education
   Barbara E. Brittingham and Thomas R. Pezzullo

2. The Emeritus Professor: Old Rank - New Meaning
   James E. Mauch, Jack W. Birch, and Jack Matthews

3. "High Risk" Students in Higher Education: Future Trends
   Dionne J. Jones and Betty Collier Watson

4. Budgeting for Higher Education at the State Level: Enigma, Paradox, and Ritual
   Daniel T. Layzell and Jan W. Lyddon

5. Proprietary Schools: Programs, Policies, and Prospects
   John B. Lee and Jamie P. Merisotis

6. College Choice: Understanding Student Enrollment Behavior
   Michael B. Paulsen

7. Pursuing Diversity: Recruiting College Minority Students
   Barbara Astone and Elsa Nuñez-Wormack

8. Social Consciousness and Career Awareness: Emerging Link in Higher Education
   John S. Swift, Jr.

1989 ASHE-ERIC Higher Education Reports

1. Making Sense of Administrative Leadership: The 'L' Word in Higher Education
   Estela M. Bensimon, Anna Neumann, and Robert Birnbaum

2. Affirmative Rhetoric, Negative Action: African-American and Hispanic Faculty at Predominantly White Universities
   Valora Washington and William Harvey

3. Postsecondary Developmental Programs: A Traditional Agenda
   with New Imperatives
   Louise M. Tomlinson

4. The Old College Try: Balancing Athletics and Academics in
   Higher Education
   John R. Thelin and Lawrence L. Wiseman

5. The Challenge of Diversity: Involvement or Alienation in the
   Academy?
   Daryl G. Smith

6. Student Goals for College and Courses: A Missing Link in Assessing and Improving Academic Achievement
   Joan S. Stark, Kathleen M. Shaw, and Malcolm A. Lowther

7. The Student as Commuter: Developing a Comprehensive Institutional Response
   Barbara Jacoby

8. Renewing Civic Capacity: Preparing College Students for Service
   and Citizenship
   Suzanne W. Morse

1988 ASHE-ERIC Higher Education Reports

1. The Invisible Tapestry: Culture in American Colleges and
   Universities
   George D. Kuh and Elizabeth J. Whitt

2. Critical Thinking: Theory, Research, Practice, and Possibilities
   Joanne Gainen Kurfiss

3. Developing Academic Programs: The Climate for Innovation
   Daniel T. Seymour

4. Peer Teaching: To Teach is To Learn Twice
   Neal A. Whitman

5. Higher Education and State Governments: Renewed Partnership,
   Cooperation, or Competition?
   Edward R. Hines

6. Entrepreneurship and Higher Education: Lessons for Colleges,
   Universities, and Industry
   James S. Fairweather

7. Planning for Microcomputers in Higher Education: Strategies
   for the Next Generation
   *Reynolds Ferrante, John Hayman, Mary Susan Carlson, and
   Harry Phillips*

8. The Challenge for Research in Higher Education: Harmonizing
   Excellence and Utility
   Alan W. Lindsay and Ruth T. Neumann

1987 ASHE-ERIC Higher Education Reports

1. Incentive Early Retirement Programs for Faculty: Innovative Responses to a Changing Environment
   Jay L. Chronister and Thomas R. Kepple, Jr.

2. Working Effectively with Trustees: Building Cooperative Campus Leadership
   Barbara E. Taylor

3. Formal Recognition of Employer-Sponsored Instruction: Conflict and Collegiality in Postsecondary Education
   Nancy S. Nash and Elizabeth M. Hawthorne

4. Learning Styles: Implications for Improving Educational Practices
   Charles S. Claxton and Patricia H. Murrell

5. Higher Education Leadership: Enhancing Skills through Professional Development Programs
   Sharon A. McDade

6. Higher Education and the Public Trust: Improving Stature in Colleges and Universities
   Richard L. Alfred and Julie Weissman

7. College Student Outcomes Assessment: A Talent Development Perspective
   Maryann Jacobi, Alexander Astin, and Frank Ayala, Jr.

8. Opportunity from Strength: Strategic Planning Clarified with Case Examples
   Robert G. Cope

1986 ASHE-ERIC Higher Education Reports

1. Post-tenure Faculty Evaluation: Threat or Opportunity?
   Christine M. Licata

2. Blue Ribbon Commissions and Higher Education: Changing Academe from the Outside
   Janet R. Johnson and Laurence R. Marcus

3. Responsive Professional Education: Balancing Outcomes and Opportunities
   Joan S. Stark, Malcolm A. Lowther, and Bonnie M.K. Hagerty

4. Increasing Students' Learning: A Faculty Guide to Reducing Stress among Students
   Neal A. Whitman, David C. Spendlove, and Claire H. Clark

5. Student Financial Aid and Women: Equity Dilemma?
   Mary Moran

6. The Master's Degree: Tradition, Diversity, Innovation
   Judith S. Glazer

7. The College, the Constitution, and the Consumer Student: Implications for Policy and Practice
   Robert M. Hendrickson and Annette Gibbs

8. Selecting College and University Personnel: The Quest and the Question
   Richard A. Kaplowitz

1985 ASHE-ERIC Higher Education Reports

1. Flexibility in Academic Staffing: Effective Policies and Practices
   Kenneth P. Mortimer, Marque Bagshaw, and Andrew T. Masland

2. Associations in Action: The Washington, D.C. Higher Education Community
   Harland G. Bloland

3. And on the Seventh Day: Faculty Consulting and Supplemental Income
   Carol M. Boyer and Darrell R. Lewis

4. Faculty Research Performance: Lessons from the Sciences and Social Sciences
   John W. Creswell

5. Academic Program Review: Institutional Approaches, Expectations, and Controversies
   Clifton F. Conrad and Richard F. Wilson

6. Students in Urban Settings: Achieving the Baccalaureate Degree
   Richard C. Richardson, Jr. and Louis W. Bender

7. Serving More Than Students: A Critical Need for College Student Personnel Services
   Peter H. Garland

8. Faculty Participation in Decision Making: Necessity or Luxury?
   Carol E. Floyd

1984 ASHE-ERIC Higher Education Reports

1. Adult Learning: State Policies and Institutional Practices
   K. Patricia Cross and Anne-Marie McCartan

2. Student Stress: Effects and Solutions
   Neal A. Whitman, David C. Spendlove, and Claire H. Clark

3. Part-time Faulty: Higher Education at a Crossroads
   Judith M. Gappa

4. Sex Discrimination Law in Higher Education: The Lessons of the Past Decade. ED 252 169.*
   J. Ralph Lindgren, Patti T. Ota, Perry A. Zirkel, and Nan Van Gieson

5. Faculty Freedoms and Institutional Accountability: Interactions and Conflicts
   Steven G. Olswang and Barbara A. Lee

6. The High Technology Connection: Academic/Industrial Cooperation for Economic Growth
   Lynn G. Johnson

7. Employee Educational Programs: Implications for Industry and Higher Education. ED 258 501.*
   Suzanne W. Morse

8. Academic Libraries: The Changing Knowledge Centers of Colleges and Universities
   Barbara B. Moran

9. Futures Research and the Strategic Planning Process: Implications for Higher Education
   James L. Morrison, William L. Renfro, and Wayne I. Boucher

10. Faculty Workload: Research, Theory, and Interpretation
    Harold E. Yuker

1983 ASHE-ERIC Higher Education Reports

1. The Path to Excellence: Quality Assurance in Higher Education
   Laurence R. Marcus, Anita O. Leone, and Edward D. Goldberg

2. Faculty Recruitment, Retention, and Fair Employment: Obligations and Opportunities
   John S. Waggaman

3. Meeting the Challenges: Developing Faculty Careers. ED 232 516.*
   Michael C.T. Brooks and Katherine L. German

4. Raising Academic Standards: A Guide to Learning Improvement
   Ruth Talbott Keimig

5. Serving Learners at a Distance: A Guide to Program Practices
   Charles E. Feasley

6. Competence, Admissions, and Articulation: Returning to the Basics in Higher Education
   Jean L. Preer

7. Public Service in Higher Education: Practices and Priorities
   Patricia H. Crosson

8. Academic Employment and Retrenchment: Judicial Review and Administrative Action
   Robert M. Hendrickson and Barbara A. Lee

9. Burnout: The New Academic Disease. ED 242 255.*
   Winifred Albizu Meléndez and Rafael M. de Guzmán

10. Academic Workplace: New Demands, Heightened Tensions
    Ann E. Austin and Zelda F. Gamson

*Out-of-print. Available through EDRS. Call 1-800-443-ERIC.

ORDER FORM

Quantity   **Amount**

_____ Please begin my subscription to the 1991 *ASHE-ERIC*
Higher Education Reports at $90.00, 33% off the cover
price, starting with Report 1, 1991.   _____

_____ Please send a complete set of the 1990 *ASHE-ERIC*
Higher Education Reports at $80.00, 41% off the cover
price.   _____

_____ Outside the U.S., add $10.00 per series for postage.   _____

Individual reports are avilable at the following prices:

1990 and 1991, $17.00	1983 and 1984, $7.50
1988 and 1989, $15.00	1982 and back, $6.50
1985 to 1987, $10.00	

*Book rate postage within the U.S. is included. Outside U.S., please add $1.00
per book for postage. Fast U.P.S. shipping is available within the contiguous
U.S. at $2.50 for each order under $50.00, and calculated at 5% of invoice
total for orders $50.00 or above. All orders under $45.00 must be prepaid.*

PLEASE SEND ME THE FOLLOWING REPORTS:

Quantity	Report No.	Year	Title	Amount

Subtotal:	
Foreign or UPS:	
Total Due:	

Please check one of the following:
- ☐ Check enclosed, payable to GWU–ERIC.
- ☐ Purchase order attached ($45.00 minimum).
- ☐ Charge my credit card indicated below:
  - ☐ Visa   ☐ MasterCard

[| | | | | | | | | | | | | | | | |]

Expiration Date _____

Name _____

Title _____

Institution _____

Address _____

City _____ State _____ Zip _____

Phone _____

Signature _____ Date _____

SEND ALL ORDERS TO:
ASHE-ERIC Higher Education Reports
The George Washington University
One Dupont Circle, Suite 630
Washington, DC 20036-1183
Phone: (202) 296-2597